CHILD ABUSE, PSYCHOTHERAPY AND THE LAW

CHILD ABUSE, PSYCHOTHERAPY AND THE LAW

ROGER KENNEDY

Foreword by Dame Elizabeth Butler-Sloss

FREE ASSOCIATION BOOKS / LONDON / NEW YORK

Published in 1997 by
Free Association Books Ltd
57 Warren Street, London W1P 5PA
and 70 Washington Square South,
New York, NY 10012–1091

ISBN 1 85343 371 3 hardback

A CIP catalogue record for this book is available from
the British library.

Produced for Free Association Books by
Chase Production Services, Chadlington, Oxon OX7 3LN
Printed in the EC by J.W. Arrowsmith Ltd, Bristol

CONTENTS

ACKNOWLEDGEMENTS

The following chapters appeared in earlier versions:

Chapter 1 in *Bulletin of the British Journal of Psychiatry* 13: 471–6.

Chapter 2 in *Bulletin of the British Journal of Psychiatry* 15: 129–32 and N. Wall (ed.) (1977) *Rooted Sorrows*, London, Jordan Publishing.

Chapter 3 in *Bulletin of the British Journal of Psychiatry* 12: 361–6.

Chapter 4 as 'Work of the day', in R. Kennedy et al. (eds) (1987) *The Family as In-Patient*, London, Free Association Books.

Chapter 8 in T. Margison (ed.) (1997) *Psychotherapy of Psychosis* London, Gaskell.

Chapter 9 in *Psychoanalytic Psychotherapy* 10 (2): 143–54.

FOREWORD

Many books have been written on the subject of child abuse from
many different perspectives over the past ten years. Few, however,
can be more informed and authoritative than this book by Dr
Kennedy. He discusses the interaction between the court, the social
work agency and the Cassel Hospital. In a chapter I found particularly valuable he explains the problems faced by troubled families
and his assessment of parenting capacity (Chapter 2). He sets out
the experience gained from the dedicated work at the Cassel with
severely disordered families and provides guidance with an extremely useful table as to those families most likely to benefit from
being sent there (Chapter 3). He gives a useful reminder of the
pressures on professionals working with disturbed families and
their need for support. There is an interesting chapter on female
abusers (Chapter 7) and another on Munchausen syndrome by
proxy and post-natal breakdown (Chapter 8). The involvement of
the courts in the assessment of the prospects of rehabilitation of
problem families is seen from the viewpoint of the psychotherapist.
The result is a fascinating and valuable book which deserves a
wider reading public than fellow mental health professionals.
Judges and lawyers concerned with cases of child abuse within the
family, as well as social workers, will find much of value to assist
in the difficult task of deciding whether the child can remain
within the family or must be placed elsewhere.

Elizabeth Butler-Sloss

1 INTRODUCTION

Those working with families in the field of child abuse often find themselves becoming intimately involved with family law. Although the involvement may produce confusion and frustration in professionals untrained in the law, it may also help facilitate appropriate and effective treatment of severely disordered families. The work described in this book is based on the assumption that the legal framework can help those working in the mental health field, and also that a psychotherapeutic understanding of individuals, families and groups can aid lawyers in steering families more effectively and humanely through the legal process. The term psychotherapy in this context refers to a body of theoretical and clinical knowledge concerned with looking at people's conflicts, feelings, anxieties and reasons for actions, which includes an understanding of the unconscious processes of the mind. A psychotherapeutic approach cannot provide a substantial basis for legal theory, for the latter is heavily weighted towards the notion of the 'reasonable' man, whose unconscious ideas and emotions are only significant if they lead to an intention to act illegally and the carrying out of the illegal act. However, the day-to-day practice of law may be enriched by a more rigorous attempt to understand human emotions, particularly in the often emotionally painful areas of family law. Moreover, there seem to be a number of shortcomings in the current complex, sometimes muddled, way that families have to deal with the law. A psychotherapeutic understanding of some of the reasons for this muddle as well as of the general issues in this field may have benefits for lawyers, mental health workers, social services departments and the families themselves, to whom this book is addressed.

The Family Unit at the Cassel Hospital, Richmond, is the only substantial medical establishment with in-patient beds for whole families, and it can provide detailed and relatively safe observation and treatment of severely disordered families. The book, *The Family as In-Patient* (Kennedy et al., 1987), describes the theoretical and clinical basis of this work in detail, but

Chapters 3 and 4 in this volume give an overview of the Unit. Among the different kinds of family treated, the hospital has had considerable experience with those who have neglected their children over years and have subjected them to one or more episodes of violent attacks. Such physical abuse, where there is a breach of what one could call the 'physical safety barrier', has occasionally been accompanied by sexual abuse and the breach of the better known 'incest barrier'.

The Cassel is a psychotherapeutic setting where the needs and rights of the child are kept to the forefront of all treatment, and this includes detailed understanding of the inner world of thoughts, feelings and play of the child. Simultaneously, the aim is to support the parents' own authority and capacity to look after their children by expecting them to take on a considerable responsibility for themselves and their children, in a relatively drug-free environment. The treatment programme consists of detailed nursing work focused on everyday family activities and parenting skills, combined with intensive psychotherapy for the parents and, if necessary, for the children. An initial six weeks' assessment is offered, followed by the possibility of about a year's treatment. Great emphasis is placed on monitoring at-risk families and making sure the children are safe. This means that when families in which there has been abuse are admitted, they initially have a strict plan around them, which limits their freedom, until some trust has built up. They are then gradually allowed more freedom and responsibility as the admission proceeds. Approximately half to three-quarters of the fourteen families at any one time in the Unit have children in the care of their local authority.

Much of the treatment of these families involves regular liaison with the relevant social work agency, frequent attendance at case conferences and occasional appearances by senior staff in court. The Unit is often used as a resource to establish whether or not a family is capable of being permanently rehabilitated. This extensive experience is used in the book to illustrate some of the complicated issues arising from the interaction between families, the law and mental health workers. In most of the families considered, the law has been invoked when a child has been severely physically and emotionally harmed by one or more of its natural or step-parents. However, by this time, the family may have reached a point of such severe breakdown that they cannot stay together as a unit, however much rehabilitation is subsequently attempted. The law at this point could be seen as offering an emergency escape route for the abused child. In other circumstances, the law may be invoked by mental health professionals at a time of family crisis in order to prevent abuse, such as by calling a case conference and asking the courts for a supervision order, and so on. The law in this case seems to provide a boundary for the professionals and the family through which the parents cannot step, if they wish to keep their children. Whether or not this manoeuvre actually helps the parents to be more effective in the long term is debatable, as there seems to be little research into the outcome of such interventions on future family functioning. One could argue that without simultaneous psychological treatment of the family, the invocation of the law does little except foster an unnecessary sense of persecution in the parents which may in the end put their children more at risk. By placing more emphasis on the parents' rights, the Children Act attempts to remedy this situation, to some extent. But this may still leave the parents feeling merely threatened, unless there is some adequate psychological help for them. As these are often difficult parents, with whom such work can be anxiety provoking and frustrating, they and their children may need skilled psychotherapeutic understanding and handling, not merely supportive counselling which does not address the very complex issues involved in these matters and the powerful feelings evoked in the families and in those around them.

It also seems to be the case that once a family comes into contact with the law, then it is exceedingly difficult for the family to be free of it subsequently; not that it is always necessary to invoke the law for all abusing families. The law, as currently organized, seems to be particularly pedestrian, at times excessively bureaucratic and most tenacious. Though a child can be rescued quickly from danger, the subsequent procedures for deciding what is in the best interests of the child can still be lengthy and cumbersome – often at a time of the child's life when his or her need is for emotional and physical certainty. Thus, what may be necessary for legal and immediate clinical reasons, may not in fact be in the long-term best interests of the child. It is not known if the delays that are necessary, while all the factors are weighed in court, damage the child and how much children can subsequently recover from any damage at this time.

In essence, the authority of the law takes over from the parents to a greater or lesser extent when their own authority as parents, and their capacity to take responsibility for their children and keep them safe from harm, breaks down. What is at issue, both in the clinical setting and in the courts, is parenting capacity, which is difficult to define. This issue is addressed in detail in the next chapter. In brief, this can be seen to refer to the parents' capacity to allow and tolerate a child being dependent on them; and to appreciate the child's world, with its need for good enough physical and emotional security, reasonable flexibility, appropriate disciplining, warmth and understanding, on a daily basis. With many abusing parents, several of these basic elements of child care have broken down; they may often feel that they cannot take on their role as parents for the whole day, for a variety of reasons, such as a lack of their own parenting, immaturity, envy towards their own children, severe marital discord and social pressures. The physical attack on their children is multi-determined. The parents often seem to be enormously threatened by the possibility of experiencing in themselves feelings of vulnerability and dependency. Attempts to do so, such as acknowledging their dependency on a partner or a professional worker, are not infrequently accompanied by acute suicidal feelings. Their children are, as a consequence, subjected to repeated breakdowns in parental affection which, if untreated in the community, may result in physical abuse as the end product of their parents' emotional precariousness. It also seems that those families who cooperate with treatment without subjecting their children to further abuse, are those who can trust, to some extent, their professional workers, and can allow specific emotional contact with them. If a family is unable to allow trust to develop in spite of appropriate help, then it is likely that treatment will fail. This does match the experience of other workers in the field such as Bentovim et al. (1988).

The issue of parental capacity has been raised, but there is also the related issue of parental authority, which essentially refers to the degree to which parents can fulfil their adult social responsibilities with regard to their children. The scope of parental authority, or 'parental responsibility', to use the terminology of the Children Act, is wide in legal terminology, and includes the following rights and duties: right to care, custody and possession; right to access; right to determine education and religion; right to discipline; right to consent to the child's marriage; right to consent to medical treatment; right to veto the issue of a passport and give consent to emigration; right to administer the child's property; right to appoint a guardian; right to agree to adoption and to consent to an application for custodianship; right to consent to change the child's surname; right to represent the child in legal proceedings; duty to secure the child's education; and duty to maintain, protect and represent the child in legal proceedings.

What the legal definitions leave out is how a parent may or

may not feel they have any authority of their own, which may in turn lead them to neglect their duties. An inner conviction of the ability to sustain being a parent usually implies a reasonably secure upbringing and a reasonably adequate physical environment for the family, neither of which may be the case for large numbers of people. Many such people seem to get by without major family disruption, but there would seem to be an increasing number of people for whom the responsibility of parenthood provokes break-down of their functioning as responsible members of the commu-nity. How such families relate to the authority of the law may be of great prognostic significance with regard to their capacity to change.

It is probably inevitable, given the law as it is currently organ-ized, and the kind of families who need legal intervention, that the law and its representatives, particularly the social work agency, are seen as persecuting external authorities. The parents frequently complain to a greater or lesser extent of a feeling of being perse-cuted by social workers, doctors or lawyers. They very rarely com-plain about being understood or looked after. Some of their com-plaints seem to be justified when there is real persecution and intimidation by any agency, as is undoubtedly the case on some occasions. And no doubt much more could be done to make the practice of family law more comprehensible to the clients and pro-vide more backing for those parents who sincerely regret what they have done and wish to change.

More often than not, however, the sense of persecution the parents complain of is a mirror reflection, as it were, of their own inner feelings of being persecuted. The feeling may be conscious but the reasons for the feeling may be unconscious. Such reasons may include the fact that the parents have frequently experienced real persecution in one form or another from their own parents, including at times physical and sexual abuse; though they may not have been abused as such as children, they may have suffered from severe emotional deprivation; and they may have had an experience of an arbitrary, punitive father. Such environmental failures may be too painful for the parents to bear thinking about, yet their own children may unconsciously remind them of their own deprivation. The birth and presence of a child are highly complex and powerful events for the adult. A child may awaken past conflicts and reopen old narcissistic wounds; the adult may be quite capable of inter-adult relations, but quite incapable of responding to the child. The child, or a particular child in a family, may come to represent the parents' unwanted bad parts. In extreme situations, the child's presence may precipitate such a disruption in mental functioning, that the child will be subject to primitive and unmodified attacks at the hands of the adult. In a sense, one could understand this attack on their children as simultaneously an unconscious attack by the parents on their own persecuting 'inner' parents, the ones who, in reality or fantasy, neglected them.

This 'internal attack' is often seen in those patients in the hospital who apparently want constant parenting, or appear very needy, and yet, in spite of considerable efforts by staff and other patients, avoid using help. Instead, they constantly bite the hand that feeds them while, at the same time, they appear quite un-aware of the aggressive aspects of their demands. The end result is that external authorities have to become parents for the children. In a sense, at least in some of the families, this is a great relief to them, and of course to the children, but the motives behind the need to take over parental responsibility and the parents' need to give up their child are not necessarily faced. Once the authorities act as parents to the child, they will to some extent arouse feelings and yearnings in the actual parents to be looked after by the authorities in a way that they did not experience as children or adolescents. Yet the parents usually fight these yearnings and deny any sense of dependency on the authorities, complaining instead of being persecuted. They may take great pains to look for any tiny loophole in the caring and monitoring structure that is around them, rather than feel relief. It is, in fact, usually persecuting and sometimes humiliating for them openly to acknowledge their dependency needs. But if rehabilitation is to succeed, and if the parents are to take back responsibility for the children, the facing of these dependency issues seems to be fundamental.

Equally important for successful rehabilitation is the capacity of the workers around a family, including legal representatives, to understand, monitor and effectively deal with the considerable *anxiety* that these families usually evoke. It is inevitable that work-ers will feel anxious about these cases; it can be even more worry-ing when workers do not feel anxious about them for it may indicate some denial of the family's difficulties or danger. The workers' anxiety is made up of various elements: they have to be at the receiving end of the family's own general anxieties, they may have to take on worry and concern for the children in the absence of parental concern, they may have to face unconsciously represent-ing figures from the family's past such as an unsatisfactory parent, and they may find that they have their own problems and anxieties touched on or stirred up by the families they meet. Professionals may deal with these pressures in a variety of inappropriate ways, if they are unaware of what is happening. They may become excessively rigid, authoritarian, punitive or collusive. They may also act as if they were similar to the figures from the past transferred onto them. Professionals need to maintain a subtle balance between protecting themselves from anxiety and being open enough to be available to deal with the family's anxieties. It is the Cassel's experience that such professional robustness requires considerable support and supervision from senior staff.

Clinical Example: The 'C' Family

This example is fairly typical of the interaction between psychotherapy and the law in day-to-day work. The treatment of mother, father and their baby daughter 'Rachel' involved a complex interplay between clinical treatment and the law, involving much frustration, misunderstanding and anxiety for all parties. When they were first seen for assessment, following referral by their social worker, they denied any difficulties, and they also denied physically abusing previous children who were removed for adoption. There seemed little that could be done at first, but on firmly taking up their denial, they then owned up to the previous abuse. However, they tended to blame the authorities in a blanket way for their difficulties. Mrs C's schizophrenic mother abandoned her at birth to the care of a punitive relative. She herself felt that she was never mothered by someone who wanted her. Mr C came across as a lonely, isolated man, prone to sudden outbursts of rage. In spite of their difficulties, both parents strongly wanted to look after their baby, who was put into care because of the abuse of the previous children and the fragility of the family situation.

In the assessment period, the couple showed some ability and willingness to engage with us in treatment and to improve in their handling of Rachel. But it was considered necessary that a particularly tight legal and clinical framework be in place in order for treatment to succeed, because of the vulnerability of the mother and the father's tendency towards delinquency. Some fostering arrangements were required for the weekend as the couple were too dangerous to have total care of their child, and a graded plan of rehabilitation was needed. However, the couple did not agree to our conditions and, through their solicitor, insisted on disputing the Cassel's view in court. On the day of the hearing, a senior member of staff found himself doing what has now become common practice: that is, helping, by means of some clinical input, two or more parties (in this instance, social services and the family) to sort out in the corridor what to present to the judge. The family seemed to have had bad advice from their solicitor, who had little idea of what the treatment consisted of and who seemed to want to take a belligerent attitude. Both barristers kept going from the Cassel staff member to their clients in order to establish what was clinically feasible and what they could incorporate in a legal order; in the end, the family agreed to the conditions of treatment. On the one hand, it seemed a waste of everyone's time to be dragged at short notice to court but, on the other, it could be argued that the parents had to see whether or not the Family Unit could withstand their onslaughts.

Although treatment went smoothly for some time, the next hiccup occurred when the family returned to court for a progress report. The Cassel was not invited to come, and was only asked for a brief report. The father used the opportunity to make the Judge impatient with the Cassel about his therapy times. The father gave the erroneous impression that he had not been given times that enabled him to continue his work, and the Judge appeared to agree with him. This apparently trivial episode put the treatment in jeopardy. The father used the fact that he appeared to have obtained backing for his actions to continue to be delinquent, frequently missing individual or marital sessions or appearing late, returning to the hospital late, and being generally dismissive and at times abusive to staff. The mother became increasingly out of touch with reality. Her therapist, in particular, felt that she was becoming psychotic. Earlier in the treatment, she had experienced visual hallucinations of the children that were removed from her. Although the hallucinations were taken seriously, at the same time it was felt that they took place in the context of her beginning to mourn the loss of the children, and that the hallucinations thus had psychological meaning. In fact, they disappeared over a period of days, without medication. Nonetheless, their appearance was indicative of a psychotic predisposition, and at the point when the legal framework was breaking down, she appeared increasingly bizarre. For example, she felt she had a special relationship to me (the Consultant), and would often give me strange meaningful looks, as if indicating that she was a particularly important patient. While the husband was not psychotic, he did not help his wife keep her hold on reality as he was so often absent or inconsistent. Overall, the rehabilitation of the family was blocked. The Cassel had tried to push ahead with the graded plan to allow the couple increasing time alone with Rachel, but the couple were much too anxious to accept these proposals.

The staff were beginning to feel quite pessimistic about the outcome by the time of the next appearance in court. A letter had, in fact, been written to the Judge to explain the reality of Mr C's therapy times and, on this occasion, a detailed report was presented, and both myself and the senior registrar attended court. Our attendance was obviously necessary in order to re-establish the conditions of treatment. In fact, although the Judge was very insightful and understood the complexities of the case, Mr and Mrs C's lawyers tried, both before the hearing and during it, to make the hearing into an adversarial contest, which came near to jeopardizing the whole framework. However, it was clear to the Judge that the Cassel and the social services department were desperately trying to help the family and were not engaged in some competitive exercise. At the same time, it was made clear to all the parties that by the time of the next appearance there had to be a definite opinion about whether or not rehabilitation was possible.

In general, it really does seem that in order for rehabilitation to succeed, what is needed is a partnership between mental health workers and lawyers. Without this partnership, the mental health workers are left with having to pick up the pieces or having to carry excessive anxiety, as was the case with this family. In fact, soon after the court appearance, in which the framework for treatment was re-established, the treatment took off again, and the rehabilitation programme advanced. The mother became more in touch with reality and her husband became much more involved in treatment. Without his cooperation a successful outcome would have been impossible, for he had an important role in providing a more realistic attitude to his daughter than his more psychologically vulnerable wife.

In this clinical example, some rather difficult treatment issues which have involved the law are outlined. They were typical of the muddled situations with which workers have to deal. The moment there appeared to be a weak point in the treatment framework, the rehabilitation of the family began to break down. My input as a psychotherapist was useful in allowing the parties to come to an acceptable legal decision. I was not looked on as some sort of strange monster speaking an alien tongue: on the contrary, I was welcomed and worked hard by the parties. The example also shows how a delicate balance has to be maintained in these cases between all the parties involved. The pathology of the families is such that they will look for loopholes in the holding structures, and, often against their own interests, attack the caretakers.

Parents have every right to go to law when they can and this is not in dispute. On the contrary, perhaps one of the Cassel's main jobs is in fact to help often relatively uneducated and/or deprived families get a fair hearing within a system in which they may feel lost. These families not infrequently find themselves repeating with the authorities their own way of relating with each other. The authorities may come to represent the family's own unsatisfactory parents, which may make the family themselves feel constantly humiliated, punished or misunderstood by those around them. They may then in turn wish to attack and punish those whom they see as responsible for unnecessary persecution. Perhaps mental health workers or lawyers do not sufficiently appreciate this kind of dilemma. However, it is quite possible that even with more appreciation of these issues by the professionals these families would continue to make those around them feel muddled, for this feeling may mainly reflect the family's own confusion and it may simply have to be tolerated by the professionals. It is certainly the Cassel's impression that a considerable part of the psychotherapeutic treatment of these families consists of tolerating and understanding states of confusion in workers and in those they treat.

One common finding in the treatment of these families is that workers may be so caught up in the confusion and uncertainty that they forget the basic principle of this work, that of keeping the best interests of the child in mind. Instead of offering a safe monitoring or treating framework, the workers' behaviour and attitudes may merely reflect the parents' pathology. In order to provide a safe professional framework that keeps in the forefront the rights and needs of the child, one could consider that there are several essential elements, including the following:

1. Clear lines of professional responsibility

It would seem to be of paramount importance for the various workers to know what they are responsible for, and the limits of that responsibility. For example, one of the main responsibilities of consultants is the admission and discharge of patients. They cannot be forced to admit someone they think is unsuitable for treatment, neither can they force a Judge to admit someone when the Judge is against rehabilitation. Workers in the Unit are always mindful that they have an enormous clinical responsibility when taking on these difficult families, and yet they are also aware that the ultimate responsibility for the child's future rests in other hands. The Unit may make recommendations, but the court ultimately decides what will happen. In practice, the courts are very keen on finding a sensible solution to a child and family problem, where at all possible; and if the Unit can be of help then the courts are usually keen to use it. The fact that there is no comparable unit regarding depth of experience and expertise, and that can offer day-by-day observations of family functioning, obviously puts the Cassel in a strong position to support rehabilitation, or to provide a strong and clear clinical opinion about the future of a child. However, the Cassel needs the backing of social work agencies as much as backing from the courts, for the Unit has to work on a regular basis with them. As these families are constantly producing tensions in the workers around them, there needs to be an ongoing relationship between workers in order to understand and process these tensions. Workers in the Cassel want the social workers to do their job, to be clear about their responsibilities and to remind the Cassel of theirs.

2. Effective communication between workers
This follows from the last point, but can only be established if different workers are clear about their roles and responsibilities. Workers in different settings, in different institutions and offices, may be skilled in working with their clients, but not necessarily skilled in working with professionals from other institutions. Effective communication may only be possible when structured meetings are arranged to examine specific issues to do with a family. If there is too much reliance on informal passing on of information, very soon there may arise considerable distortions in people's perceptions of each other and in the nature of the information itself. The passing on of information is facilitated if there is a clear focus of work agreed upon by all parties.

3. Promoting mutual trust
It is the Cassel's experience that successful work with these families depends on a process of trust developing between the families and the network of professionals both within our setting and outside it. However confronting we may have to be with the parents, if the confrontation takes place within an essentially trusting context, then change in the parents may take place. The two previous points imply that the workers have to develop trust in one another for treatment to be effective. But work with the families should also take place with the assumption that workers are trying to develop a trusting relationship with them. These are often families where trust has broken down between the parents, and between the parents and the children. In addition, many parents have never had an experience of a trusting

relationship. One could argue that there is all the more reason to offer them the opportunity to make an intimate emotional contact with professional workers, in order to help them work through some of their previous disappointments.

In the following chapters, the aim will be to discuss in more detail the issues raised above concerning the assessment and rehabilitation of multi-problem families. There will be consideration of the assessment of parenting, the details of the Cassel treatment programme, some specific clinical conditions, as well as mention of some of the Cassel's research findings. In addition, there will be an examination of some specific issues concerned with the mind of the abused child and the abused adult. Often with this kind of work one has, as it were, to 'bear the unbearable'. What is meant by this is that in the treatment of abused and abusing families, time and again the staff and the families are called upon to bear unbearable experiences, traumatically painful experiences of abuse which the immature child cannot and could not deal with. By helping the children and their parents to bear these difficult experiences, to find words to express their distress, we hope to enable them to take charge of their lives, rather than continue to be the victims of their past.

2 ASSESSMENT OF PARENTING

Assessing and treating families in which there has been severe child abuse is anxiety provoking and stressful for professional workers. There is a need to keep the children safe, to establish where possible a working relationship with the parents and, at the same time, to confront the often severe family pathology, especially where there is the possibility of change within the family. Each one of these aims can provide enormous difficulties for the professional, and where all three have to be maintained simultaneously, the task can feel overwhelming. Making judgements about what should happen to a family, whether or not children should remain with their parents or be separated from them permanently or temporarily, and trying to assess the potential for rehabilitation are very complex and difficult tasks. What is presented is based on the author's fifteen years of working with problem families at the Family Unit of the Cassel Hospital. The Unit has built up extensive experience of undertaking the arduous and occasionally nerve-racking task of rehabilitating families for which other forms of treatment have either failed or have been insufficient.

The 'applied' and fairly eclectic psychoanalytical approach described may provoke a certain amount of scepticism; indeed, it would be suprising and even a little disappointing, if it did not. The aim is to show, through detailed argument and the use of clinical illustrations, that such an approach can address the difficult inner worlds of disturbed children and their parents, while also being in touch with the complex issues of child care and child protection. The use of family therapy, behaviour therapy, the occasional use of psychotropic drugs, and anything else that may work with difficult families is not ruled out. The advantage of the Cassel environment is that there can be a combination of sophisticated psychotherapeutic work and more confrontative work around everyday living issues with families, particularly through the nursing. It can also be argued that the advantage of an analytic approach is that it is particularly useful in the treatment of intractable problems, because it is a form of therapy that by its very nature aims to tackle directly destructive and negative behaviour.

The danger of using naive and untrained or inexperienced coun-
sellors is that they may be so caught up with a wish to see the
best in their clients that they have missed their clients' destructive
side, which may have been directed at their vulnerable children.
Not that it is necessary to look only at the negative side; obviously,
a balanced approach is wisest. However, it is often difficult for
workers in the field, especially when they have put in a lot of work
with a family, to maintain their objectivity; so that they may find
themselves swinging either too much against or too much in
favour of parents, while forgetting the needs of the children.

When dealing with problem families, child mental health workers
are constantly being asked directly or indirectly to assess parenting
capacities. Courts and social services agencies often wish to have an
opinion about the ability of parents to look after their children, keep
them safe and to attend to their physical and emotional needs. With
the troubled family, one can see how parents may wish to give up
their responsibilities to professionals and ask for parenting themselves. They may give up their children, or be tempted to do so, even
when offered treatment. They may fight off attempts to help them, or
may feel that they cannot face the responsibility of being a parent for
the whole day. The responsibility of parenthood may provoke a
breakdown in the parents' functioning, making them unsafe to be
with their children. Some parents may be very confused about how
much responsibility they can take for their own emotions, how much
should be kept between adults and how much may spill over into the
children's lives. Such confusion may result of course in physical,
sexual or emotional abuse of the children, in which the children's
needs and interests come second to those of the adults.

Though there is much that is still not understood in this field and
though the practical task of making judgements about the future
behaviour of families is complex, difficult and often confusing, there
would seem to be three essential questions that are raised time and
again when family assessments of such problem families take place.

1. What is meant by good enough parenting, and how is parental
   capacity assessed?

2. When are children safe to be with their parents and when is it
   best to remove them?

3. When should a problem family be given the chance to stay
   together, despite major problems, and when should treatment be
   abandoned?

A thorough assessment of parental capacities or, to use the terminology of the Children Act, of parental responsibility, is the basis for providing answers about questions of childrens' safety and the chances of successful treatment outcome. At the Cassel Hospital there is a severely disordered population of families for assessment and treatment; yet the issues raised by tackling such families highlight, admittedly perhaps rather starkly, issues relevant in other assessment and treatment settings. Before tackling the clinical issues directly, there will be a general discussion about parental responsibility, followed by an outline of some main criteria for assessing parental responsibility.

PARENTAL RESPONSIBILITY

The Children Act defines parental responsibility as 'all the rights, duties, powers, responsibilities and authority which by law a parent of a child has in relation to the child and his property' (s. 3(1)). However, the Act does not define in any detail the nature of these rights, as the list, it is argued, would be constantly changing to meet different social situations. The issue about the relationship between social attitudes and the practice of family law is complicated. The courts cannot isolate themselves from society, nor on the other hand do they wish to be seen too often to be in advance of social attitudes. Taking marriage as one example from the family field: in the 1950s, it was considered relatively abnormal for a couple to live together without being married; but by the 1960s and early 1970s, judges recognized that this situation had significantly changed and that cohabitation was an acceptable way of life for families. Similarly, attitudes, at least in the courts, to one-parent families have also dramatically changed. There is a much more tolerant, flexible and pluralistic attitude to the nature of family life. Family lawyers are increasingly beginning to realize that there is a need for them to be more informed about child care issues, and for them to keep abreast of research as well as different practices in other countries. However, there is still usually an assumption that the ideal family for a child involves having a loving mother and father, and that this view is maintained by the majority of the population. It is, indeed, difficult to avoid promoting values of one sort or another in this field. But even if it were believed that it is better for a child to have an actively involved father and mother, it is obvious that their mere presence does not guarantee adequate and effective parenting. For this reason, and because we need to answer specific questions about problem families, there is a need to be specific about the nature of parental responsibility, even if definitions have to change as society changes. But because of the difficulty, if not impossibility, of avoiding value judgements, it is probably important to attempt to find criteria for looking at parenting issues which can be applied to a variety of different family constellations.

What seems to be common, and perhaps not too controversial, to most theories of human development, is their stress on how the relationship between parents and children changes as the child grows. It appears to move from one in which there is absolute dependence on the child's part, to relative dependency; or from close, primary ties to the parents to a situation in which these ties are loosened over time. As the responsibility for their children changes, so the children's responsibility for themselves changes. There is a constant and shifting relationship between the parents' and the child's responsibilities. A good enough parent probably needs to recognize these shifts, as indeed do we all, including the media. It is noteworthy how often events involving children, such as those involving acts of violence perpetrated by children, are seen as either all the children's fault, or all the fault of the parents, rather than something which has involved a difficulty in the relationship between parents and children. It is worth noting that the House of Lords ruling on the Gillick case concerned an under-sixteen's right to have contraception against her parents' wishes, provided that she was capable of taking some responsibility for herself and could understand what this involved. Thus the law at that point found common ground both with the findings of child development and with the changes in contemporary society, which had been leading to increasing recognition that parents no longer had total control over their children. The landmark nature of the ruling was that the law recognized and made specific children's rights and the limitations of parental rights, introducing the notion of developing responsibility. Though the judges were right to emphasize that young people can take responsibility for themselves, it is perhaps worth emphasizing that very young children also have a right to be dependent on their parents and not to be responsible prematurely.

Theories of human development also have their own stated or implied theory of human agency, concerning reasons for actions and the nature of human freedom. For example, each theory tries to address how much freedom children have, or should have, in relation to their parents. Most theories seem to state that as the child grows up, there is a need for the caretaker to allow the child increasing freedom to explore and to discover him or herself, within a reasonably secure environment. But there are also some very difficult issues involved: for example, how much freedom to act children may be allowed; how parents may foster children's freedom to think while, at the same time, offering limitations on their freedom to act; and the issue of how parents can allow children a life of their own, by offering some kind of model with which they can identify, yet which can allow them to find their own way to conduct themselves. There is probably a need for parents and children to be actively negotiating such issues as the children develop. It is certainly the Cassel's experience with problem families that very often the children are seen as mere extensions of the parents, with little life of their own. Much of the therapeutic work is aimed at changing the parents' perceptions of their children, so that they are no longer seen as mere objects to be used or abused, but as separate and living beings whose identity should be respected and fostered.

In general, parental responsibility could be seen to consisting of the following conditions: the parents, or parent, need to provide a reasonably secure physical environment, given limitations on income and social conditions. They need to have the child's needs and interests to the forefront of their thoughts and actions, to allow the young child to be dependent on them, and to allow the developing child increasing freedom and autonomy. They need to appreciate the child's world, with its need for good enough physical and emotional security, reasonable flexibility and appropriate disciplining which does not lead to physical abuse, and warmth and understanding on a daily basis. Parental responsibility involves taking responsibility for one's own emotions as an adult, and not exposing the child to adult sexuality which may lead to sexual abuse. It implies accepting the reality of the child as a separate life developing in his or her own way, but needing guidance and some structure. Parental responsibility also involves recognition of the need of the child gradually to take on more responsibility, and that there is a shifting relationship between child and parental responsibility.

MAIN CRITERIA FOR ASSESSING
PARENTAL RESPONSIBILITY

Perhaps the main overall criterion for assessing parental responsibility is the willingness and capacity of parents to take appropriate responsibility for their actions. If parents constantly blame others for their own failings, or if they blame the courts and the social services for all that has gone wrong in their family, then the chances are that the prognosis for change in the family is poor. It may be difficult to be precise about degrees of responsibility, but the capacity of parents to own up to their negative thoughts and actual negative and destructive actions sets the tone for any detailed assessment of their parenting.

Particularly difficult judgements about degrees of responsibility arise when assessing a parent who has not actively carried out abuse of a child, but has been indirectly implicated. Of course, parents may be relatively blameless in such circumstances, particularly if they have acted swiftly and effectively and taken appropriate action to make sure their children are safe. Sometimes the 'passive' partner in abuse has been so physically intimidated by the 'active' abuser that he or she has been unable to seek help. Assessing these situations is fairly easy. But it is the more subtle circumstances that make for difficult assessment judgements. There may be, for example, a mother who has turned a blind eye to what has been going on in the home, and has not been able to notice severe bruising of her child. Clearly, by any ordinary criterion, this is evidence of parental neglect. The prognosis for treatment of such a mother will depend critically on her admitting that she was at fault and being willing to accept help. Parents who repeatedly blame their abusing partner for all the abuse, and who cannot see that their own blindness was part of the abusing situation, are very difficult, if not impossible, to treat. Sometimes the complicit partner has only a limited memory of what has taken place in the home, either because of alcohol or drug intoxication during the incidents, or because the memory has been repressed as too painful to bear. A series of interviews in the context of a therapeutic relationship may be necessary to get to the truth of the matter, and before the parent can have access to the memories, particularly when they have been repressed for emotional reasons. Though it may be important to reconstruct the events which led to the abuse, it may not be possible to know all the details at once. Sometimes it takes months to find out what really happened. Usually, it would seem to be enough that one has a basic understanding of the events, with a certain amount of detail, particularly when the parent is willing to admit fault and to seek help.

Other aspects of the assessment of parental responsibility include the following major areas of concern:

1. Adequate provision of physical care, including being physically present for the child
This is usually the easiest capacity to assess, as it can be seen by a home visit and by pooling of evidence from outside observers,

including nursery and school staff. But the presence of physical care alone is, of course, no guarantee of good enough parenting. A child may have a comfortable bed, but an adult may be sexually abusing the child in it.

2. Consistency of behaviour and functioning in regard to the child
This includes providing appropriate and safe boundaries for the child, respecting the child's own world, perceiving the child as different from the adult and with different needs, and providing appropriate restraint of adult needs and impulses. It entails the parent keeping the children in mind, particularly when they are vulnerable and in need of a parent. It probably also involves some capacity to function as an adult, to be able to socialize with adults and not expect a child to take the place of adults for the parent, so that the children do not become little adults. One would expect the parent to have reasonable impulse control, not to expose the child to criminal, delinquent and destructive behaviour. If a parent cannot keep a child safe, then parental responsibility has broken down. Under this heading, one could include states of mind which may impair parental responsibility to a greater or lesser extent, such as acute psychosis. Some parents may lose the capacity to parent temporarily due to illness, but may recover it once they are better.

Where there are two parents, it is of course essential to assess the quality of their relationship. Particular areas to focus on include how much they can communicate between themselves, and how much they use their children as vehicles for communication; their capacity to talk to each other about difficulties; and their capacity both to support one another and yet to retain independence. Collusive partnerships, in which an abusing parent is backed up by the other partner despite clear evidence of abuse are, of course, particularly worrying. One needs to assess the degree to which the collusion is maintained when challenged.

Grey areas include circumstances when children have come to harm when not in an adult's care, for example, if they have been left to play with other children in the road or at a playground. The media repeatedly draw attention to tragic circumstances when a child had been abducted and/or murdered while away from their parents. One may ask, at what age can a child be left to play unsupervised? While not willing to provide rigid answers to this question, perhaps one could say that in this day and age, most children of primary school age should have clear guidelines about what is or is not acceptable about where they should play, with whom and for how long they should be absent from their home.

Merely allowing a young child to go out to play, without clear expectations about what is acceptable, may be very risky in contemporary society.

3. Capacity to empathize with the child

One would expect the parent to be able to understand the child's needs and wishes, though the parent may need help in this area, particularly with adolescent children who tax most parents' patience. Empathizing implies not expecting the young child to take responsibility for the adult, though unfortunately it is not uncommon for children to feel they are responsible for what goes wrong in a family. Emotional liability or flatness in parents may interfere with their empathy for the children. Empathy includes a capacity to put oneself in the child's shoes, to try to feel what the child feels. This is different from imposing what the parent feels on the child, or not allowing the child to have any sense of being separate from the parents.

In the assessment of empathy, one would look at how parents respond to a child's emotional and physical pain, whether or not they express love and concern, or rejection and hate, and the degree of ambivalence. With mothers and babies, one is particularly looking at the quality of the bond between parent and child, the capacity to keep the baby in mind for the whole day, and to provide adequate intense physical and emotional care.

4. Capacity for trust

A major indicator of parental responsibility is the parent's quality of relating, both in the family relationships and in the relationships between the family and the professionals. It is the Cassel's experience that successful work with problem families often depends on a process of trust developing between the families and the network of professionals. These are families who have been enormously threatened by the possibility of experiencing feelings of vulnerability or dependency, with the result that their vulnerable and dependent children have been subjected to neglect or abuse. A useful indicator of parental responsibility is the degree to which the professionals feel that they have to take on responsibility for the child. If many professionals are working endlessly around a family in the hope that the family will benefit, and if the professionals are pouring in emotional and financial resources, it is often the case that the family is not engaged in significant work with the professionals, who are in fact taking over from the parents. Workers close to a family may need supervision in order to overcome entanglement in the family pathology. This can happen when the workers are over-involved and over-identified with the family, as much as when the workers have an over-negative view of the family.

A capacity for play may be an important indicator of a reasonable parent–child relationship, even when other indicators are negative. Such a capacity indicates sufficient trust and intimacy between the child and parent. Woodenness in play, or totally confused play, may be indicative of poor parenting, especially when combined with one or more of the other criteria of parental responsibility.

5. Capacity for change

This would seem to be a crucial area of assessment, involving all the various aspects of parenting. In the end, if parents can change their attitude and behaviour, despite major difficulties, then obviously there is more hope that they can become more effective parents. But judgements about change are difficult to make, and may require observation over a period of time. It has already been suggested that a developing capacity for trust is an important prognostic factor. One may add here the need for some developing capacity for insight and a shift in the quality of their relationships, particularly in the relationship with the children.

6. Historical factors

Many parents who have difficulty taking on parental responsibility have had deprived childhoods, and a number of them have been sexually and/or physically abused as children. Never having been truly allowed to be children themselves, some of these abused adults are compelled to harm their own children. But historical factors in themselves may only indicate risk factors. Not all abusing parents were abused as children, though the great majority have had emotionally deprived upbringings. In particular, a number of problem parents have had major adolescent problems. Instead of having had an opportunity to grow gradually into adulthood through the transition period of adolescence, they have resorted to premature sexual behaviour, or have left home early to escape from family difficulties, or have become parents very early and before they were emotionally ready for parenthood.

7. Behavioural criteria

Using each of the above categories, it may be important to focus on specific behavioural criteria of parental responsibility for each family undergoing assessment. For example, it would be important to assess how a family coped with everyday tasks such as eating, sleeping and playing with the children, and then correlate their behaviour with emotional factors. One may look at how consistent and safe their behaviour was in these situations. Observations in an out-patient clinic alone may not really show up the family's day-to-day functioning. It may be important to make observations in the home, or the foster home where appropriate.

8. Pooling information

It is often necessary to pool information about problem families from a variety of sources, including from social services, mental health workers, general practitioners, health visitors, paediatric facilities, schools, nurseries, play groups, relatives, friends, neighbours, the police, the probation services and the courts. Sometimes it is necessary to meet the relevant workers before making an assessment in order to clarify essential details and to get a feel for the professional relationships. One has to weigh up the usefulness of such a prior meeting against the possibility of prejudging the issues before actually seeing the family. I personally prefer where possible to see the family first for myself. I like to focus on the quality of the relationships between the parents and the children because, in the end, that is what will determine what happens to the family. It is surprising how often I am expected to do an assessment of a family without the children. I virtually never agree to doing an assessment without seeing the children with the parents. Without observations of what actually takes place between them, one may be fooled into being too optimistic or pessimistic about the parents' capacities. Subsequently, one may have to see the workers, including foster parents, in order to match up one's own observations with those of other professionals.

CLINICAL EXAMPLES

Making judgements about parenting capacities is in the end a complicated matter, involving the fitting together of a number of different elements including direct observation of the family and information from other workers. An attempt has been made to indicate the main areas on which to focus but, in the end, it is the total picture that has to be kept in mind, and that is often a very difficult task, given the often extreme anxieties aroused by problem families and the many details about their current and past lives that have to be examined. One has to avoid trying to explain everything about a family's current life by means of their past, because one may avoid the current issues of safety to the children. Yet, at the same time, it is obviously important to have some understanding of what went on in the past, in order to assess what might happen in the future. The following examples are from three difficult assessments, which are designed to highlight the complexity of this work, as well as to give some guidance in an often confused and anxiety provoking field. Some treatment issues are also tackled because it is often difficult and indeed unrealistic to sharply distinguish assessment from treatment, as the assessment process involves looking at the capacity to change and to respond to treatment. In addition, treatment often involves continuing assessment of parental responsibility, based on several or all of the elements outlined above.

Example 1: Mr and Mrs A and daughter B

These parents, in their mid-twenties, had mild learning problems. Their nine-month-old daughter had been removed from them following non-accidental injury at the age of six months, when the parents presented at casualty. Mother was apparently the perpetrator. The child was placed in a foster home, and care proceedings were begun. When assessed by a specialist unit, there was great worry expressed about the parents' capacity to look after their child. Mother, in particular, seemed quite inept in her handling of the baby. Father, who was better with the physical care, was very angry with his wife. The couple hardly communicated, and there was not much hope that they could have their child back. On the other hand, mother was full of guilt and remorse about what had happened, and the couple were desperate to have their child back. They cooperated with the social services' plans, including keeping up regular access visits.

When the family was seen, what was striking was the quality of the remorse, which seemed genuine enough. But there was a certain amount of ambiguity about the injuries. Mother insisted, when pressed, that the trouble had been that she had let the baby's head hit the pram. She denied that she had thrown the baby across the room onto the wall, as had been suspected from the nature of the injuries. Although there were considerable doubts about the couple's capacities, it was thought worthwhile to admit them for a six-week assessment, in order to test out their capacity to change and to find out more about the abuse. It was arranged that they would be admitted first of all without the baby, in order to settle in. The baby, who went home for most weekends to the foster parents during the admission, was then admitted after about a week. At once, the couple showed how dependent they were; they made themselves homeless on the day of admission, and we had to insist that they find accommodation, in this case a bed and breakfast hotel. Although both parents were immature and needy, there was some benefit in the fact that they moved out of a difficult family environment, the home of the paternal grandmother. Indeed, it was revealed that the abuse took place in the context of a difficult relationship between Mrs A and her mother-in-law. Mr A's loyalties were very divided, and he came across as very unsupportive to his wife.

At first, Mr A took over the care of baby B, while mother was very clumsy with her. But soon this situation changed in that she became more confident, and indeed the baby started to flourish and look well, despite the fact that the fostering arrangements broke down and another foster family had to be found at short notice.

The severe pathology in the couple's relationship soon became evident. Mr A revealed a history of violence, going back to his rather delinquent adolescence. He showed a great lack of trust in his wife. On the other hand, he doted on his daughter. Mother felt, from early on in the pregnancy, that the husband was only interested in her being pregnant in order to have his child, not for any other reason. She had become the receptacle for a number of his projections: for example, that she would be unable to keep the foetus safe. His daughter represented for him the ideal baby that could overcome all his own childhood damage.

In our assessment, it was clear how difficult it was to come to a clear decision about the possibility of rehabilitation, as it was still not clear how much the parents were capable of changing in order to be effective parents for their daughter. It was felt that it would not damage the baby to extend the assessment for a further period, particularly in view of the fact that the fostering had been interrupted. Staff were particularly surprised that the baby had flourished. This could not be accounted for simply by being in a supportive environment; it does require the mother in particular to be providing something good for this kind of phenomenon to occur. But staff were not happy to go ahead with treatment. Instead, it was proposed to reassess the family and to have clearer answers to the following points. More was needed to be known about the abuse. The mother kept backing off from fully admitting to her violent impulses, which clearly took place in the context of both a difficult marriage and a difficult family environment. Staff were quite suspicious about the father's role. He came across as a man seething with rage, but who could hardly dare admit this openly, except when it concerned his wife. The couple needed to be more engaged with others in the hospital and to be less dependent on them.

The next period of assessment, in fact, quite soon gave a much clearer answer. After an initial period of unrealistic euphoria from the mother, who believed treatment had been recommended when in fact the situation was still uncertain, the true picture became clearer. In a sense, nothing new was learned, in that the couple did not shift. Mother maintained that the injuries were essentially accidental, and the couple were unwilling to budge from that story. In addition, and crucially, the baby rapidly lost weight. We acted quickly and removed the baby back into the foster home during the week. The next assessment meeting was difficult, particularly as the parents were routinely present during the meeting; but it was clear that rehabilitation was not possible, and that the baby needed to have a permanent placement, preferably adoption. Due to its young age, it was likely that there would be no access to the parents after the adoption.

One might ask why the assessment took place at all, given the obvious parental difficulties. After all, there were problems in most of the areas outlined previously. The mother had difficulty providing basic physical care of the baby; she could not play with the baby; there was a basic unwillingness to own up to the injuries, given the medical and forensic evidence; the marital relationship was very difficult, with intense mutual projection processes; and the couple did not readily trust professionals. In answer to this, it was true that there were always great doubts about the couple's capacity for change. But the workers felt it important to test this out. Indeed, at first, it did seem that this was a wise decision, in that the baby began to flourish. But clearly our caution was correct. The change was not sustainable; perhaps because the mother did not want the baby. In fact, it was quite noticeable that once her daughter was removed from the hospital, she herself began to brighten up. Treatment was offered to the couple, for which funding became available, but the father in particular did not wish it. The couple left the hospital together and apparently united, but angry with the hospital for having made our decision.

Example 2: Mrs D and daughter E, aged three
This single mother, in her twenties and diagnosed as having Munchausen syndrome by proxy, administered a household substance to her elder daughter until she nearly died. The child was removed permanently, but the mother, who was on a probation order, was admitted to the Cassel with the younger daughter for assessment. At first, the mother was aloof and showed little

capacity for empathy with her child, whom she treated like an object; and she showed little remorse for what she had done. She soon became enraged when challenged, and it was felt that there was little chance for rehabilitation. At the out-patient assessment, there had been some signs of empathy with the child and some willingness to seek help, but that had apparently changed on admission. Mother used the child for comfort, often sleeping with her at night. On most of the outlined criteria, this mother seemed to fail to show the necessary degree of parental responsibility. However, just before the formal assessment meeting was due, it was made clear to her that as things were she was unlikely to be offered help. This produced panic, and then the sudden revelation that she herself had been subjected to repeated sexual abuse as a child by a family member. Though sceptical at first, the allegation was taken seriously and appeared to be genuine. The revelation coincided with her suddenly showing a more vulnerable and less aloof side to her character, which in time made her more amenable to treatment.

However, treatment was difficult and stormy at times. The essential parenting issues had to be constantly kept in mind. Mother showed a supersensitivity to separations from her daughter, who continued to live at a foster home until staff felt more able to trust the mother's capacities to empathize with the child. Mother seemed at times to be near to disintegration when near to expressing feelings of dependency. At other times, she would go into omnipotent and bullying states, when she believed that she had the right to do what she liked to herself and her daughter.

Assessment of her mothering capacities was a constant and ongoing process, and very much part of the treatment process itself. Slowly, in treatment she began to develop a capacity to feel for her daughter's state of mind as well as her own, that is, a capacity for empathy. She also began to tolerate and express her aggression towards staff, other patients, and, particularly, her experienced male therapist. What seemed to become clearer in the therapy was that she had little inner maternal representation; the image of herself as a mother was very damaged and fragmented. It seemed a crucial piece of work when she was more able to acknowledge her critical, poisonous side. She was then more able to present a more integrated sense of identity. She seemed less fragmented as a person and coincidentally less dangerous to her child. Her daughter, meanwhile, appeared to become more robust and less caught up with her mother. There are still concerns some years after discharge, but mother is more trusting of professional help, and has made considerable progress.

Example 3: Mrs E and son A, aged 10

Mother, in her late thirties, was diagnosed as schizophrenic. She and her son were referred in order to clarify whether or not she could look after her son permanently, or whether he should remain in his long-term foster home. The boy, who had been removed from her care a couple of years previously because of her mental state and mothering difficulties, was placed in a foster home where he was subjected to sexual abuse. He was then placed in a safe foster family, but obviously there was major concern about what had happened, and the local authority, who were being sued by the mother, felt that they had to make every attempt to look into the family situation and to fully assess the mother's capacities to care for her son in the long term.

Mother had a long psychiatric history. As a child, she was severely sexually abused. Her mother was a prostitute and the patient was involved as a child in pornography. She spent much of her childhood in care, and was also sexually abused in foster care. She began to cut herself around puberty and, as a result, she was placed in a variety of residential placements which could not contain her. She finally ended up in a secure unit. She had a history of alcohol and hard drug abuse, and was eventually diagnosed as schizophrenic. She suffered from auditory hallucinations and delusions, and had periods of acute breakdown requiring acute admission. She had also lost several children because of her problems.

On admission, she was on depot injections of major tranquillizers. In the six-week assessment period, mother was cooperative. In individual therapy sessions, she came across as mechanical, emotionally cut off and fragmented at times. However, as the admission proceeded, she was able to express more of her anger about the abuse of her son, yet she also maintained an unrealistic view of her capacity to look after him. In small group sessions, she was, in contrast, surprisingly able to relate to the others and the situation, becoming at times the most insightful member of the group. But, in general, she was only just able to hold herself together by means of nursing and patient support. She was out of touch with her child's needs. She described how she needed him in order to 'keep her boundaries'.

Her son was able to use the therapeutic setting well. He expressed in moving terms, in his individual sessions, a deep sadness and a wish for stability. Memories of the sexual abuse kept breaking through. He was happy in his foster home, but also fond of his mother, and wished to continue to see her.

Owing to the mother's great difficulties in being in touch with her son in a realistic way, it was clear at the assessment meeting that rehabilitation was an unrealistic option. Instead, we offered to do focal work with both of them to help them to say goodbye; but with the additional aim of helping the mother to be able to maintain some limited access to the foster home. Until then, access had been unrealistic as she had been angry with, and suspicious of, the foster parents.

A further four-month period of treatment with the mother was begun, while the son returned to the foster home. There were a few meetings with the son, and the mother and son together. We also facilitated meetings between mother and foster parents. This was a very difficult time for the mother. She felt drawn to her world of violent destructiveness, with drink, drugs and sexual promiscuity. She began to hear voices and to break down. However, her major tranquillizers were increased for a while, and were able to keep her going through this period. She found a 'voice' for herself with the other mothers, and also established a good relationship with her nurse. She became able to talk more realistically in therapy sessions about her own abuse, her wish to destroy men, and her ability to get into abusing relationships with the world, including social services. By discharge, she had a friendly relationship with the foster carers, and arrangements were made for regular access visits. Her son was also able to see how unrealistic it was for him to live permanently with his mother, and further therapy was arranged for him.

Treatment was successful because we kept to a focal task as a result of the assessment. We were not aiming to cure the mother, but to help her deal with the specific issue of letting her son go. The process of allowing separation in this instance required in-patient treatment because of her constant pull towards psychotic breakdown. In her own words, she needed her son to keep her sane. Without the hope of him being there for her, she began to break down again and thus needed in-patient holding.

DISCUSSION

The three clinical examples presented involved particularly difficult assessments. However, the three questions raised earlier informed the decision-making process. In each case, we had to answer the question of whether or not the children were safe with their parents and whether or not to recommend treatment, once we had established as far as possible the quality of the parents' relationships with their children. In the first example, despite signs that the parents might change enough to become safe, in the end they were unable to do so. They continued to deny their responsibility for the abuse of their daughter, and the mother could not in the end bear to be close to her child. The mother in the second case was able to reveal a more human and vulnerable side, once the reality of her own childhood abuse was revealed. In the third case, we were able both to recommend continued removal of a child and, at the same time, to offer a therapeutic opportunity for both mother and child, despite the mother's severe pathology.

Each assessment opens up complex and difficult clinical and, indeed, social issues. In making these assessments, workers hope to be acting in the interests of the child; but they also come up against society's problems, expectations and dilemmas concerning the nature of the family. An approach has been presented that can be applied both rigorously and humanely across different social and ethnic conditions.

There have been times when the Cassel's recommendations have been diametrically opposed to the opinion of social services. Sometimes the Cassel has been proved right; sometimes the social services have been proved right. Sometimes it is difficult to distinguish between occasions when one group of professionals is holding something important in the case, for instance, a necessary degree of scepticism, and occasions when they are being prejudiced. The rehabilitation of one case at the Cassel was held up for nearly two years because of the opinion of a social services department, and needed the intervention of an independent expert and a High Court case before our own opinion carried the day. However, these situations are happily fairly rare. Though there may be differences of opinion, most situations can be resolved provided professionals are willing to make time to get together to share information. Just meeting in a room can almost of itself be therapeutic to a case. However, it is also the Cassel's experience that over-sceptical social workers under pressure to keep budgets tight can overlook real potential in a family.

So often misperceptions and negative fantasies about other workers dominate the workers around families. For example, not infrequently workers, particularly lawyers, think that the Unit is rather harsh to patients because so much is expected of them. They are so used to hearing complaints about the hospital that they are often taken aback when they actually visit and rather like being on the Unit, and even find it friendly.

The Unit's own research findings in general match the experience of Great Ormond Street Hospital (Bentovim, 1992), which has divided assessment of outcome into hopeful, doubtful and hopeless, depending on the degree to which parents take responsibility for what has happened in the family, whether they can recognize their children's needs, and the quality of family attachments.

The research (Fonagy et al., 1996) has, so far, shown that parents who have experienced abuse as children, but who show a capacity for self reflection during assessment and treatment, are able both to deal more effectively with their abuse and to show evidence of change in their parenting capacities.

Other research on the treatment programme (Healy, et al., 1991; Healy and Kennedy, 1993), has indicated that families benefit from treatment when their parent or parents can remember at least one good childhood relationship; when they own up to any abuse; and when they can engage in a reasonable treatment process, in which the child and the parent–child relationship can be attended to.

Making effective assessments is obviously a vital part of work in the child care field, for it is on this basis that decisions as to the future of a child are made. This chapter has tried to indicate specific areas of parenting that need to be looked at in any assessment.

A main issue in any assessment and treatment of the problem family is how to encourage parents to take on parental responsibility once they have partly or totally given it up, while not taking over from them. It is particularly difficult for the professional to stand by while a parent is actively rejecting a child, or is not relating well to a child. The professional usually wants to intervene and prevent the child from suffering. While this attitude is understandable and may be essential, there are also times when it is just as important to stand back and allow the parents to discover, or recover, responsibility rather than take it away. In treating problem families, there is a constant tension between the need to intervene and the need to foster responsibility by not taking over. In order to have an effective assessment of the degree to which a parent can change, it is necessary for workers to be able to see when they can stand back and when they simply have to intervene. This is not an easy task, especially these days when anxieties about being negligent abound and when time for the assessment and basic facilities is in short supply.

3 THE CASSEL FAMILY UNIT AT WORK

The Family Unit at the Cassel Hospital is the only substantial and long-established medical establishment with in-patient beds for whole families, and it can provide the opportunity for detailed and relatively safe observation and treatment of severely disordered families, as well as abusing cases. A number of different kinds of family are treated, including those in which a mother has suffered a severe post-puerperal breakdown, those in which one or more members of the family have a severe psychiatric condition such as chronic depression or Munchausen syndrome by proxy, as well as families whose whole functioning in many aspects of life has broken down.

OUTLINE OF THE TREATMENT PROGRAMME

A comprehensive description of the Family Unit treatment programme is already published in the book *The Family as In-Patient* (Kennedy et al., 1987), with detailed clinical descriptions of the treatment of children, adults and whole families. Up to fourteen families are admitted at any one time for six weeks' assessment followed by the possibility of treatment for up to eighteen months. It should be emphasized that the Unit admits only those families where other kinds of treatment, including family therapy, drug treatment and intervention at school, have not succeeded. That is, we take the most seriously disturbed families, within certain limits. We do not aim to treat patients suffering from acute psychosis; nor do we accept drug addicts, severe alcoholics or major crime offenders, all of whom we have so far found unable to use our resources, or else have a very destructive effect on the patient group. In addition, the safety of the children in the hospital has to be considered.

The programme, which does not usually include the routine use of psychotropic drugs, consists of detailed nursing work focused on everyday family activities and parenting skills, combined with twice-weekly individual psychotherapy for parents and, if necessary, for children. There is also a once-weekly formal, small group therapy for parents and a weekly group for older children. Family meetings with nurse and therapist take place regularly to integrate nursing and therapy. There is a focus both on family living skills and on individual needs and difficulties. The aim is to restore families to their communities so that they can continue with life unaided or at least use their local resources more effectively. The combination of working with the whole family and providing a setting for detailed understanding of the individual parent and child offers the opportunity of making close observations of the nature of family breakdown. It also facilitates a thorough assessment of a family's strengths and failings, including the risk of further abuse. It is often difficult to assess the risk without such close observation over some weeks and, for this reason, the Unit is frequently asked by social work agencies, the courts and other professionals for help in this way.

There are perhaps still misgivings that bringing children into a psychiatric unit would expose them to malign influences which could seriously affect and emotionally harm them. These fears are not borne out by events. On the contrary, on admission, many children begin to blossom when they are relieved of the burden of trying to meet their disturbed parents' emotional demands which they are not equipped to provide, or because they then receive the attention to their needs which their parents were unable to provide. Monitoring and using information about the child, him or herself, as opposed to the child created by parental needs, is another advantage of in-patient treatment. Furthermore, by expecting the father, where present, to be admitted, we aim to set great store by attempting to integrate the whole family, as so often the family's problems are caused by disturbance between couples. Breadwinners are generally expected to continue their employment, even when admitted.

Great emphasis is placed on monitoring at-risk families and making sure the children are safe. This requires both detailed attention to what is happening to the family in the Unit day by day and considerable liaison with the relevant social service agency.

Safety of the children in the hospital is maintained in a number of ways. There are various settings in which to see, hear about or discuss patients, such as daily meetings with patients, daily staff meetings and regular reviews and supervisions. Safety is also maintained by a network of staff relationships, from the nurse and therapist of a particular family, to the on-call duty team at night and at weekends. For the network of relationships to provide a secure 'holding' environment, there needs to be clear and effective transmission of information between the workers. In addition, each family will have its own particular focus of work, and a nursing plan and a primary nurse. Thus, early in admission, an abusing family may well have fairly severe constraints on their freedom; for example, they may not be allowed out of the hospital unaccompanied, until staff feel able to trust them. If treatment proceeds successfully, the constraints will gradually be reduced and the progress of the family monitored by reviews as well as planning meetings with the relevant social work agency.

In general, there are five basic elements to treatment in the Family Unit, which can be summarized as follows:

1. Active participation of the parents is expected; their capacities and difficulties are looked at but they are expected to take on responsibility for their actions rather than rely on drugs.

2. There is a special relationship of the patients to the hospital. The latter provides a physical structure in terms of the bricks and mortar of the building and its layout. This structure is looked after by patients and nurses: for example, in daily work groups which involve cleaning and maintenance. This allows patients to feel they are taking an active part in the life of the hospital.

3. The hospital provides sophisticated therapeutic structures. These include psychotherapeutic talking treatment undertaken in consulting rooms; nursing work which takes place in group and individual settings, mainly though not exclusively around activities; formal meetings for patients and staff; and supervision of the therapy and nursing. In addition, patients are involved in the life of the hospital community, which consists of their active participation in and taking responsibility for such things as cooking teams, washing-up rotas, and baby-sitting.

4. In order to provide a framework for registering events in the Unit and for making sense of what takes place, the Cassel believes that effective transmission of information about patients is needed, as well as staff sharing of strains, and considerable support and supervision by the senior medical and other staff.

5. The rights and needs of the child are kept to the forefront of all treatment, and this includes detailed understanding of the inner

world of thoughts and feelings of the child, including understanding of their play. For this understanding to be skilled and effective, the input of the child psychotherapists attached to the Unit is essential.

The Family Unit sees its role as not only to take on very difficult families for treatment, but also to provide a resource for other workers in the field to use where appropriate. One of the Unit's main tasks is often to help other workers clarify their own positions with difficult families as well as offering an opinion on what we think is going on in the family. In addition, we feel we have the knowledge – through seminars and conferences with senior workers, administrators and others involved in the mental health field – to help clarify the complex issues raised by abusing families and other seriously disordered families.

SUMMARY OF OBSERVATIONS OF CHILD ABUSE

Although work on child abuse is widespread (see, for example, Bentovim et al., 1988, for a review) there remains a number of important gaps in our knowledge of the nature of abuse and of the personality of the abuser, its long-term effects and the effectiveness of treatment programmes. The Cassel's own preliminary findings can be divided for convenience into general and specific features.

General Features of Severe Family Breakdown

In common with multi-problem families with no actual observed or reported abuse, this group displays general features of the breakdown of family life. In simple terms, these include the following characteristics: draining the financial and emotional resources and the patience of primary care teams and then specialist organizations; breakdown in ordinary, everyday activities so that basic events like organizing meal and bed times cannot take place effectively (see Chapter 4 for more detail of this issue); diffuse psychiatric symptoms such as chronic depression and anxiety in one or more parents; general symptoms in the affected children, including emotional or conduct disorders; and the inability of the parents to feel confident about keeping young children and babies in mind over vulnerable and critical periods, such as night-time or in situations of danger and risk, such as boisterous physical activity. The last feature implies that families with these characteristics who may not immediately come to the notice of authorities for severe abuse may, however, be on the edge of abuse.

Specific Features of the Abusing Family

We have repeatedly found that the parents do provide some caring for their children, but it is often only of a 'partial' kind. Other workers have described the frequent presence of 'role reversal,' where the child is treated as if he or she were an adult, while the caretakers expect satisfaction of their own desires to be cared for. But in addition the abusing parent, and often the partner where there is one, can only give 'divided' attention to the child who subsequently becomes the victim of abuse. This partial orientation reveals itself as the inability to fix on the needs of the child and to perceive his or her emotional pain. It is paralleled by the parents feeling enormously threatened by the possibility of experiencing in themselves feelings of vulnerability and dependency. Frequently, when one examines the timing of physical attacks on the children in consultations, one discovers a recent episode which has evoked in the parent the threat or the possibility of experiencing dependent feelings.

The risk of this occurring is most clear in the Family Unit for in-patients around weekend separations from the hospital. Patients are expected to return to their homes for weekends, unless there is a crisis or something for them to work on in the hospital. Accounts given by the patients towards the end of the week often reveal them feeling threatened by having to experience dependent feelings towards the hospital. They may describe an 'unbearable' psychological pain and may also become a suicidal risk. Looking back over the pattern of attacks on children with these families, Cassel staff have noticed how the expression of these feelings in the adult is soon followed by the threat, and sometimes the reality, of some kind of attack on the child, though such attacks in the hospital are rarely severe enough to warrant legal action. One hypothesis is that the existence of such feelings and severe attacks on their children are causally related. As a result of these observations, workers on the Unit have become more easily alerted to the risk of abuse.

Two factors in the history of these patients seem, in addition, of particular significance for understanding the nature of the disturbance. First of all, the parents may have had an experience of being parented as children, but there has been the absence of what one could call a 'fixed' relationship to the parents. A mother or father, or even a parental substitute, may have been present, but the patient has experienced them as never having been 'central' to them, or never having provided central attention. As other workers have described (Martin, 1980: Trowell, 1986), there is also usually a history of violent attacks on the child who subsequently becomes an abusing parent. Previous formulations have attempted to explain abuse by the fact that the abusing parent was abused as a child. However, this explanation does not take into account the fact that many parents who were treated violently as children do not become child abusers. One could speculate that it is the presence of the further factor of the lack of a fixed parental figure that tips the balance towards them becoming abusers.

But there may be a further necessary factor which has predisposed the parent to difficulties in coping with violence and depression, and that is a disturbed and difficult adolescence. Many of the abusing parents left home early as a result of conflict with their parents, and then had had a stormy adolescence with episodes of acute depression. Several parents had promiscuous sexual relations at this time; others attempted to deal with their adolescent problems by a premature first marriage which soon broke down. Some of these points are illustrated in the clinical examples. The impression, which needs to be tested by research, is that there was often a threat of an adolescent breakdown, which was warded off by various environmental 'false' solutions of the kind just outlined.

There have been many descriptions of the immediate disturbance to the children as a result of suffering abuse (for example, Martin, 1980; Lynch and Roberts, 1982; Trowell, 1986; Bentovim et al., 1988, Bentovim, 1992). But few of these descriptions take detailed account of the child's own world of thoughts and feelings. Nor has there been adequate detailed study of the effects of treatment and what features are prognostic of a successful outcome. The Cassel's findings so far agree with other workers, in that the general effects of living in a chronically abusing family are multiple, including school failure, depression, sexualization of behaviour and psychosomatic symptoms. It seems difficult to define more specific features. The impression is that there is a tendency for these children, like their parents, to mask their emotions. The child appears to hold onto the idea of a 'marvellous' parent who needs protection. There may be a compulsion in the older child to provoke more parental abuse. The child may also have the greatest difficulty in seeing the parents as 'bad' in any way, thus in fact making it difficult for them to recover from the trauma of the abuse.

CLINICAL EXAMPLES

Case 1: Mrs A and six-year-old 'Louise'

Mrs A, in her mid-thirties, was admitted in the mid-1980s with Louise for possible rehabilitation following episodes of physical abuse by the stepfather with Mrs A's complicity. The child was a Ward of Court, and the Cassel was given considerable responsibility for the case by the High Court. Mrs A had no memory of her father. She suspected that her mother was a prostitute, since there was a succession of men in the house at night, and she and her siblings had to look after themselves. On occasion they would have nothing to eat unless they managed to pawn something. She lived with an aunt when her mother disappeared when she was six. She hated the aunt who beat and starved her, while spoiling her own son. After a year, she was obliged to rejoin her mother and 'stepfather' and lost contact with her sister of whom she was fond. She ran away to London when a young adolescent and soon married for 'food and security'. The marriage broke down and she abandoned the children of this liaison. Then began a series of embattled relationships with men who were heavy drinkers and violent, including the father of Louise. She saw her daughter as a reflection of herself, a lonely and damaged child, but found great difficulty providing both physical and emotional care for her. Louise herself presented as inhibited, unable to play and inarticulate. Her Wechsler Intelligence Scale for Children – Revised (WISC–R) score was 76.

As a result of fifteen months' treatment, Mrs A was able to provide adequate and safe caring for her daughter. The major change in her seemed to be that she was more able to experience feelings of depression without feeling either hopelessly suicidal, or criticized for being, in her own words, a 'bastard', or without trying to deny she had any problems at all. The fact that she was able to see the consultant (myself) as an available authority figure who would not condemn her but would both stand up to her anger and hopefully understand her, seemed also of great importance. She was not able to blame 'authorities' outside the Unit but had to grapple with myself, the consultant, more directly. Louise gradually came to life, was able to play more and express aggression without fear of retaliation. Her WISC–R near discharge was 100. Finally, a major event occurred when Mrs A's boyfriend, a more suitable partner than previously, agreed to be admitted for the last part of the family's treatment, and he became a more benign and non-abusing father figure for Louise. Out-patient follow-up continued and the social worker in the case was supervised by us for two years until the care order was removed. Our rough estimates concluded that we saved the tax-payer at least £150,000 in fostering, legal and medical costs by investing an intense input of resources in the Unit.

Case 2: Mr and Mrs B and baby 'Jean'

The parents, in their early twenties and their eight-week-old baby, were admitted with the cooperation of the local social services department, for possible rehabilitation following episodes in which the father seriously bruised the baby, which was then put into care. The marital problem came quickly to the fore. Mrs B had little trust in her husband whom she would constantly denigrate. Mr B wished to be a 'perfect' father but was intensely jealous of the attention received by the baby. He wanted his wife's undivided attention. His own father had died, when he was a young child, of presenile dementia. He remembered him as forgetful, inactive and in need of care, while mother was stretched by the demands made by the father. Mr B remembers being a difficult child to control and often left to his own devices. He left home as soon as he could, had many jobs and affairs, and became an excessive user of alcohol and cannabis, until his marriage.

Mrs B's own parents, from abroad, divorced when she was young. Her father was constantly unfaithful to her mother. The latter was described as depressed and unavailable to Mrs B. Baby Jean was named after a loved elder sister of Mrs B. Mrs B left school early and came to England. After a period of being lonely and depressed, then having an affair with an older man, she met her husband. Admission revealed severe mothering difficulties, in that Mrs B was disconnected from the baby. She wished she were a good mother but revealed little warmth to the baby or to her husband. She feared any show of dependency on either him or the staff. She stuck rigidly to an inappropriate feeding pattern and, when bathing Jean, left her in the cold. She was withdrawn and suspicious, with little ability to focus her attention on the baby. When the original abuse had occurred, she chose to leave her baby in hospital and return to the husband in order to be furious with him rather than stay and look after the baby. Rehabilitation was attempted slowly but, in spite of some progress, broke down when the father gripped the baby too hard and bruised her. This coincided with the period when the Cassel and the social services department had agreed to proceed with rehabilitation. Contrary to expectation, this produced a massive reaction of hostility to all the workers from the parents. Once again, Mrs B chose to leave the baby with the authorities.

Case 3: Mrs D and 'Simon'

Mrs D, in her early twenties, was admitted some four years ago expecting her second child, Simon. Her first child had been put into care for adoption as a result of severe physical abuse for which Mrs D and her husband were both responsible. It was feared that the same fate would befall the next child. Following the entry of the first child into care, Mrs D attempted suicide by setting fire to the marital home. Pregnant again, Mrs D wished to end the marriage and was motivated for help with her relationship to the new baby, as she felt she had never been attached to her first child. Simon was born while she was an in-patient at the Cassel, and was immediately put on a place of safety order, followed by a full care order, with the full cooperation of the local social services department.

Initially, Mrs D gave the impression of being a somewhat wooden doll, with mechanical responses. She experienced considerable difficulty in having to participate in hospital events, and viewed staff interest in her as a persecution, particularly with regard to her handling of Simon. She revealed considerable difficulties in separating from him. Related to this was her inability at first to recognize and therefore deal with Simon's and her own dependency needs. It was seen as progress when she was able to express her irritation with Simon without excessive anxiety and without the fear of harming him. Mrs D described her own mother as an obsessional woman whose main concern was to keep the house tidy and who allowed little expression of feeling. Mrs D left the home at the age of sixteen following a row with her mother and soon married the father of Simon.

Treatment focused on Mrs D's mothering skills, helping her to promote Simon's development; on helping her face the reality of the abuse of her first child; and on fostering in her a different, more positive, attitude to the expression and understanding of emotions. Treatment was a success, and was particularly helped by a close working alliance with her social worker. On follow-up, some three years following discharge, Mrs D and Simon were well established and the care order on him had been removed.

COMMENTS

As emphasized before, judgements about suitability for treatment of these abusing cases are difficult to make. If they were made on traditional grounds, such as motivation, willingness to cooperate, capacity to make a 'therapeutic alliance', and strength of personality, then it is likely that none of these families would be treatable. It is unclear what would be the consequences of not treating these families. It is likely that a significant number of children would come to more harm. It is probable that without intervention many children would suffer from long-term emotional disorder and a proportion of these would end up, as they often do anyway, occupying places at special schools and becoming increasingly pushed onto the margins of society. In the absence of reliable long-term studies of this group of patients, it is not possible as yet to go beyond these impressions.

There is another pressing short-term problem: how to assess which families respond best to treatment, and what criteria there are for suggesting which families can be trusted to cooperate in treatment without abuse. The Cassel's past formal research on mainly physical abuse (Healy et al., 1991) revealed that open admission of abuse and the ability to remember good relationships from childhood were important prognostic factors in the successful treatment of these families. The quality of relationships established by mothers throughout their lives was identified as a factor within family functioning that was predictive of ability to engage in treatment. Good relationships remembered by the mother from her childhood increase the likelihood of establishing good relationships during treatment. Further research by Healy and Kennedy (1993) looked in more detail at which families benefit from in-patient psychotherapy at the Cassel. The findings are summarized in Table 3.1.

As in the previous study, what seems to determine the success or otherwise of treatment is the quality of relationships established by the parents. The Unit is currently engaged in more detailed research into the nature of abuse as well as the effectiveness of our treatment programme. So far, it has been found that the parents involved in emotional, physical and occasionally sexual abuse show on admission great difficulties in their capacity to reflect on their past and present experiences. Those parents who improve during treatment show a changed capacity for self-reflection (Fonagy et al., 1996) and this seems to be matched by their improved relationships with their children. The abuse seems to have had major

TABLE 3.1: Which families benefit at the Cassel

Likely to benefit	*Less likely to benefit*
Older parents with older children	Younger parents with younger children
Mother living with partner	Mother living alone or with a disturbed partner
Contact with fewer agencies	Contact with multiple agencies
Clarification regarding abuse of a child in the family	No clarification regarding abuse of child
Maternal history of affective or neurotic disturbance	Maternal history of ECT
No maternal history of childhood abuse	Maternal history of 1. Childhood sexual abuse 2. Death of a parent 3. 'In care' as a child 4. Disturbed adolescence
Focus of work on disturbance of child or of parental relationship	Focus of work on disturbance of father
Admission for more than 8 weeks	Admission for less than 9 weeks
Evidence of engagement in treatment	No evidence of engagement in treatment
Maternal 'good relationships' remembered from childhood or developed with staff or developed with patients	No 'good relationships' remembered from childhood developed with staff or developed with patients

Source: Adapted from Healy and Kennedy, 1993.

effects on the capacity of the mind to remember the past and to make emotional sense of experiences. More research is also under way into the effects of treatment on the children's development. This is an area that is lacking in comprehensive research findings. In Chapter 9 there is a summary of some of our clinical findings on the abused children, but much still remains to be clarified.

4 THE BREAKDOWN OF EVERYDAY LIFE

WORK OF THE DAY

In the previous chapter it was mentioned that the ordinary activities of daily life usually break down in the severe multi-problem family. This chapter will focus more specifically on the nature of the breakdown of everyday life in such families. To help make sense of what happens, one can use the notion of the ordinary 'work of the day' around which family life actually takes place, and which at the Cassel becomes the focus of both the psychotherapy and the nursing work. The concept of the work of the day does not refer to everything that happens in the day, but only to those events which are significant in some way to the individual and his family, or have precipitated some kind of thought process and/or action. Thus, the work of the day would include unsolved problems, major worries, overwhelming experiences, undigested thoughts, forbidden or unsolved thoughts, what has been rejected and suppressed and what has been set in motion in the unconscious by the activity of the preconscious and consciousness. It refers to all the significant and, at times, deceptively indifferent, thoughts, feelings and experiences that have occupied us during the day, and which provide the raw material for thinking and for dreaming. The work of the day is what gives material for thoughts and provides the basic framework of living.

Much of this work normally carries on automatically without the subject being particularly aware of its occurring or of its 'everydayness' and without his giving it much attention. It is normally taken for granted and yet such work is far from being simple in nature, as one can see from the treatment of disturbed families and individuals where such basic work has broken down. The work of the day is normally focused around essential activities and events such as eating, sleeping and working. Such events, often ritualized and structured to a varied extent, provide the emotional context that drives practical life. Our reliance on everyday structures and rituals, however sophisticated, to hold us together may have something to do with the nature of our emotional life, and the fact that feelings in particular are often fleeting. Because of this, we seem to need to have something solid and relatively unchanging to help us pin feelings down in order that we may acknowledge or study them. It would seem, then, that a major task of the work of the day is, as it were, to enable us to 'discover' our emotions through ordinary events. Such events, which often appear trivial, form common human intercourse and provide the basis for intimacy. Indeed, one could say that true intimacy between people often consists of being commonplace with each other without feeling awkward.

Normally, one performs the activities of the day without thinking about their basic structure; rather, the basic structure provides material for thinking; but, in the patients being considered here, the things most people do without thinking are charged with emotion and conflict and this involves the breakdown in continuity and consistency of daily life. The life of the day is then not 'held together' but begins to break down. One could also describe this in Winnicott's terms as a breakdown in the family's holding environment.

There are some similarities between what is called here the work of the day and the place and function that Freud ascribed to the day's residues and waking thoughts in the formation and interpretation of dreams. Freud emphasized the importance of recent events and the relevant waking thoughts in making a major contribution to the instigation of dreams. The significance of recent events and fresh impressions has not had so much time to be lost through the processes of repression. The instigating agent of a dream is found among the experiences which the subject has not yet 'slept on', that is, they are often undigested experiences. Freud described how the material that has occupied us during the day dominates the dream, and how one can understand dreams as a continuation of our waking life. Displacement and the use of indirect representation are mainly responsible for the dream's puzzling appearance which disguises this continuity. Freud wrote that the 'analysis of dreams will regularly reveal its true, psychically significant source in waking life, though the emphasis has been displaced from the recollection of that source onto that of an indifferent one' (1900, p. 177). In addition, Freud wrote that the day's residues 'have the most numerous and varied meanings; they may be wishes or fears that have not been disposed of, or intentions, reflections, warnings, attempts at adaptation or current tasks and so on' (1913, p. 273). The day's residues are thus the psychical material for the dreamwork to act upon. The unconscious wish is the essential additional factor in the construction of the dream. This wish can come to expression in the day's residues and can supply them with a force which enables them to press their way to consciousness. Particular unconscious conflicts can be, as it were, 'hooked' or 'transferred' onto the recent material, and the latter can provide a point of attachment for such conflicts. Similarly, one could say that the unconscious weaves its connections around the work of the day. In psychoanalytic treatment, one may be looking for past conflicts through the processes or reconstruction and interpretation of the transference, and yet one hopes very much that one is working with fresh material from recent events, that is, from the work of the day, as such material has not yet been bogged down by the processes of repression and is often rich in content. Indeed, one could go so far as to say that as long as the present and the ordinary events of a patient's life are in the treatment, one can more easily uncover the repressions of the past. As Freud demonstrated in 'The Psychopathology of Everyday Life', (1901) one is often led from the commonplace to the psychically significant, but one can also emphasize the psychical significance of ordinary events, not only as a point of attachment for unconscious conflicts, but in their own right as the framework for living.

THE BREAKDOWN OF THE WORK OF THE DAY

The Cassel Hospital provides a unique opportunity for looking at the day-to-day, week-to-week, living together of families. The families treated are in general in an extreme state of breakdown and are often barely able to cope with the ordinary tasks of living together. During the assessment procedure there is an attempt, among other things, to look at how families bring their own pathology and their 'living space' into the hospital, that is, how they bring in pieces of their reality and repeat their breakdown within the hospital. This breakdown, both in an individual and his family, could be seen as a piece of inner reality that has not stood up to social reality, and when there has been a conflict between the family and their milieu. This is obviously repeated on admission to the hospital in one way or another; however, it takes different families different lengths of time for this repetition to occur. It seems to have a time course of its own.

There are many factors leading to family breakdown. These will include individual factors such as a strained important member of the family who may have an individual breakdown or illness; or, there may be group factors in the family, that is, the family may not function effectively as a family group. There may also be chance events or important life events; and there may also be developmental factors; for example, the challenge to a family's functioning or the maturing of an adolescent child. One often finds in such families that the work of the day has broken down in the outside world and that ordinary tasks are not given enough attention. When this occurs the family, and particularly vulnerable members of the family, may well be subjected to overwhelming anxieties. The work of the day may break down when there has been severe social stress or when there has been 'malignant splitting' in the family, that is, a repeated and intense use of primitive splitting mechanisms in the family's object relations, common to most of the families we happen to treat, and which interferes in a major way with the family's capacity to attend to normal functions; or a breakdown of the normal social barriers, for example, when there has been sexual abuse by one member of the family of one or more other members.

Although the Cassel deals with a wide range of both individual and family psychopathology, one can make the general point that in a number of these families one can see a breakdown in the process of working over or metabolizing thoughts and feelings from hour to hour, day to day and from week to week. That is, there is a breakdown in the day's structure that provides the material for thinking and enables the subject to discover his or her feelings. Normal events are then experienced as persecuting and lacking in continuity, and thinking about them is painful and useless. The physical and psychic 'bricks and mortar' of the family home become loose and fragmentary, and the capacity to keep partners and children in mind becomes eroded. There appears an increasingly wide gap between the parents' knowledge about family life and their capacities to use this knowledge. Some families reach such a point that they seem hardly to be able to give their attention to events such as organizing meal times or bed times; in addition, they often resort to impulsive actions as a way of trying to get the environment to respond to their needs.

As is well known, one often finds that one or more parents of such families have suffered from fairly severe childhood emotional or physical deprivation. In more theoretical terms, one could speculate that there has been an absence of the primary infantile experience of satisfaction, what Freud called the 'bedrock of psychic life' (1900, p. 602). They seem to have experienced a repetitious absence of satisfaction as a result of parental or social deprivation. They often try to seek some satisfaction but in unsatisfactory ways. For example, many deprived patients feel both very damaged and desperately needy, and have a hope or a fantasy that the damage done to them can be totally made up; but this may lead to them desperately looking for resources, for example from professional workers, but never feeling anything is good enough. They thus tend to drain the patience and capacities of those who try to help them and so end up repeating the absence of satisfaction which they were apparently so desperately seeking to avoid. It is noteworthy in this context that we often find that a family, on admission to the hospital, is in severe financial debt, with a related housing crisis.

On this topic, one can describe at least two kinds of debt. First there is the debt in which one owes something to someone and it has to be repaid: one could call this a negative, owing debt. Second, there is the positive debt, in which one is indebted to somebody and there is no need to pay back what one has received. One could perhaps see a negative debt in families when there is a rigid repetitious link with a deprived past, that can in fact never really be paid back or done away with, that is, when there is always an overdraft to the past; whereas a positive debt obviously refers to an experience of effective parenting and is linked to some hopeful prospect about the future, when there is some kind of positive balance in the family's resources.

In the members of the families being described who, to all intents and purposes, have never had much basic experience of satisfaction, rational thinking has, in Freud's terms, never come to 'safeguard' the primary processes. Freud wrote that 'the substitution of the reality principle for the pleasure principle implies no deposing of the pleasure principle, but a mere safeguarding of it: a momentary pleasure, uncertain in its results, is given up, but only in order to gain along the new path an assured pleasure at a later time' (1911, p. 223). However, with the families we treat, there is often a fantasy that thinking interferes with their life and is both persecutory and unhelpful. Putting the situation simply, the patients then avoid the possibility of acknowledging any distress and of allowing themselves to have thoughts. In addition, there may be a turning to an inner, precarious fantasy object or to a desperate attempt to make the external object fit in with the inner fantasy object; there may also be sometimes a turning to 'alternative resources' such as drugs or perverse sexual excitement. What such patients do to their objects can also be seen as an aggressive attack on the internal parents. This latter attack may be contained in the symptoms; for example, an attack by the parents such as through neglect may be encapsulated in the patient's symptoms as an attack on the parents. This could also be seen as turning a passive childish experience into an active adult one. This is often seen in those patients in the hospital who apparently want constant parenting or appear very needy and yet, in spite of considerable efforts by staff and other patients, avoid effectively using hospital structures or any kind of outpatient psychotherapy. Instead, they constantly and desperately bite the hand that feeds them and, at the same time, seem unaware of the aggressive aspect of their demands. Such patients are well described by Main in his classic paper, 'The Ailment' (Main, 1957).

Another major theme, central in trying to understand the origin of the breakdown of the work of the day, is how the parents in these families often feel they cannot take on their role as parents, at least for the whole day. This may occur for a variety of reasons – such as a lack of their own parenting, immaturity, envy of their children or social pressures. One could in general say that the birth of a child and the existence of children are complex and powerful facts. A child may awaken past conflicts and reopen old narcissistic wounds; the adult may be quite capable of interadult relations, but quite incapable of responding to the child. One often sees in families in the hospital how difficult it may be for some parents to keep separate and intact their adult capacities and ability to respond to their children, on the one hand, and, on the other, their own child-like dependency needs. In extreme situations, the child's presence may precipitate such a disruption in mental functioning that the child will be subjected to primitive and unmodified psychic or indeed physical attacks at the hands of the adult, who can no longer distinguish the child from the unwanted bad parts of him- or herself. The child may also become the object which unites or divides a family and then becomes, as it were, a 'child object' for the family, a mere function and not a person.

WORK AT THE CASSEL

The work at The Cassel Hospital with families involves a unification of psychoanalytic psychotherapy and psychosocial nursing. In general, one could say that the hospital pays particular and focal attention to the work of the day in the total treatment of individuals and families. It becomes the focus for the detailed work of analysing sources of disability and distress. There is particular attention paid to what happens during the day at events such as eating, feeding of babies, night-time, small groups of patients and nurses doing tasks such as cleaning, and structured meetings. The achievements and conflicts from day to day and from week to week around these events become a central focus of attention. Neuroses, like dreams, have a preference for belittling the importance of the details of working life and neglecting them to the realm of the indifferent. As Freud wrote 'every neurosis has as its result the forcing of the patient out of real life' (1911, p. 218). However, the Cassel Hospital focuses on these details, and all the penumbra of resistances, denials and associations and material that occupies the hospital during the day becomes a main agent of treatment and hopefully of change; and it is hoped that such material provides the focus or, at the very least, the background for both the individual psychotherapy and the detailed nursing work. Severe splitting mechanisms, common to many of the patients treated at the hospital, have the tendency to obscure individual emotions and conflicts. For this reason, particular emphasis is placed on the details of what has happened to particular individuals and what they have experienced; what work the nurse and therapist of a particular patient are doing; as well as the nature of the particular nurse/therapist relationship (James, 1984). At the same time, there are a number of different group activities in the hospital. The group has certain useful functions; for example, it may serve as a mediator of projections, as well as the unique source of information of unconscious processes. In general, through individual and small group supervision, staff meetings and in particular the supervision of the relationship between the nurse and the therapist of particular patients, the aim is to provide a setting for self-reflection and for the registration and understanding of distorted communications and distorted relating. At the same time, as Alan Wilson wrote, 'the psychotherapeutic community is not a stable, a polite society: it is a prescription of uncertainty. Free association, but free association observed with focal attention' (1987, p. 63).

The hospital does not, on the one hand, provide rigid rules nor, on the other hand, does it believe in the free-for-all of unbounded chaos. It aims to provide daily structures for uncertainty and indeterminateness to be tolerated and worked with. In particular, in our treatment of families, the aim is to work with and support the parents' capacities. It is our experience that there are a number of disturbed families who need in-patient treatment because such basic daily work has massively broken down in the outside world, making them no longer viable as a unit. The main aim is often to enable such families to recover or discover their capacity to deal with the 'bricks and mortar' of their physical and psychic home. To a greater or lesser extent, such therapeutic work may be more important to these families, at least at the time of their admission, than more traditional understanding of the psychopathology of the individual members, although this work also usually continues during admission.

SHORT EXAMPLES FROM VARIOUS FAMILIES

The following examples attempt to show how essential activities in the families' functioning can be interfered with.

Example 1: The 'A' Family: Feeding Time

This family was admitted as an emergency following a domiciliary visit, the problem being that the mother was suffering from a severe post-natal depression after the birth of her second baby girl. Mrs A was depressed, distraught and said that she felt unable to stay in her own home. Although the birth was satisfactory, Mrs A said that she only managed to bottle-feed baby A after two months. The baby had difficulty taking anything from the bottle and would cry as if in anger. The mother described this supposed failure at feeding as the trigger of her problems and she started to feel anxious, panicky, inadequate and tearful, with increasing intensity until admission when the baby was five months old. 'I feel so guilty,' said Mrs A, 'I'm not giving her what she wants, I'm not special to her, after all anyone can give her a bottle.'

The crisis point was reached when Mrs A lost control and shut herself in the bedroom screaming, not able to deal with baby's crying. She felt she was on a knife edge, feeling afraid of losing control and afraid of slipping into madness and, at the same time, feeling it would be nice to regress to a child-like state and to be looked after. Mrs A was able to respond quite well to both her children, but separately. There were major problems at feeding time, when she seemed unable to cope with the two children together. In addition, the two-year-old would rush around at meals, trying to get mother's attention; indeed, when Mrs A was breast-feeding, the older child would writhe around on the floor screaming all the way through. Mr A, in general, felt redundant and unable to support his wife in the way she felt would be adequate. This made him feel angry, but he was unable to express this anger. Most of Mrs A's anxieties were increased at feeding times. They included a feeling of wanting to run away, thoughts of disappearing in a puff of smoke and suicidal preoccupations. She felt trapped when the baby wouldn't feed and it made her feel inadequate and over-whelmed by the demands on her. While disappointed at giving up breast-feeding at two months, she was also concerned at her own weight loss. In therapy sessions at first she disclosed how closely she identified with the baby and said how she wished to become very much like a little girl herself and admitted that she wanted to be held, cuddled, fed and looked after.

The first area of attention in treatment was the mother–child relationship, with particular emphasis on the feeding as so many of the family's problems seemed to arise at this time or, at any rate, to be increased in intensity. It is interesting that as treat-ment proceeded, Mrs A revealed her own 'feeding' difficulties; for example, a predominant feature of the family's early admission was the feeling of deadness that they provoked and evoked in other people. There was a massive denial of feelings of attach-ment to the hospital and to each other. Anything we offered the family was not accepted as good enough, while Mrs A arranged for a special kind of vegetarian meal and managed to arrange to have her meals before the other patients, which seemed to be indicative of increasing social isolation in the hospital. She then revealed in detail a number of sadistic fantasies in relation to the baby. The family became outsiders in the Family Unit and un-popular, they would not accept help as of any use and constantly maintained the idea of discharging themselves in a month's time. They maintained this idea, in fact, for a number of months.

Staff found that they were being intimidated by Mrs A's threats to leave, and exploited by her demands to be given very special treatment. While staff were disagreeing with each other, the family seemed to be doing very little in the hospital. How-ever, when this fact was realized by the staff and then put back to the family, the treatment began to move. There was consider-able work done on the theme of mourning and on the marital difficulties, as well as work with the children. When a staff member produced the concept of presenting to the family a 'stay-ing date' rather than a leaving date, the treatment turned the corner. The family settled down to detailed work and there seemed at least to be a reasonable 'feeding' relationship between the family and the hospital, and they were considerably improved on discharge and at follow-up.

Example 2: The 'B' Family: from Crisis to Crisis
This family was particularly hard to treat as Mrs B, the only available parent, had great difficulties in all areas of the work of the day. The family consisted of Mrs B and her three children of mixed race – a boy aged six and two girls aged four and five. Mrs B presented as if there were no severe problems. However, these periods of apparent calm were punctuated by repeated crises which made it impossible for work to continue on an out-patient basis with several different agencies.

A main problem seemed to be the boy who was administering medicine to his younger sisters and, on two occasions, the children had to be taken to hospital. The boy's behaviour was also difficult at school where he had become miserable, apathetic, uncooperative and unable to concentrate; in addition, he had also begun to soil. On consultation the family was quite chaotic, with the children trying to run wild while the mother sat back passively.

Mrs B showed a very inconsistent attitude to the children, particularly with the boy with whom she found it difficult to assert her own authority. When she saw her inconsistent efforts to be obeyed fail, she resorted to physical violence and then felt very guilty and afraid of being overwhelmed with anger and afraid of battering the boy to death. Mrs B and her son seemed locked in a projective system, in which he intended to represent the bad unwanted parts of his mother. Mrs B's own father was alcoholic and rejecting and had taken a number of overdoses, while her mother was weak and inconsistent. Her mother died when she was thirteen and Mrs B then ran away from home. She and her siblings were not infrequently physically beaten.

It was particularly difficult to define a focus of work for the family after the initial assessment. Mrs B presented as mindless and not knowing what to do with her own children, although well able to look after other people's children. This feature of mindlessness, which at times seemed calculated, persisted throughout the admission. Instead of thinking about what to do, she tended to get other people to think for her, by her acting out. She would often impulsively return home, causing the children considerable distress and confusion. Typical of her attitude was the way she dealt with a bill for her water supply at home. The water had been turned off by the Water Board as the bill had not been paid for three years. Mrs B expressed surprise as she had assumed that social services had been paying it automatically, in spite of her having had many reminders. Rather than negotiate with the authorities or with professionals, she wished to remain in the hospital over the weekend, because there would be no water at home. When this idea was challenged, she said that it did not matter anyway as she had a way of turning on the water without the authorities knowing – which she apparently succeeded in doing. She displayed little anxiety or insight about the episode, which was typical of many similar ones.

The episode illustrates: (a) her tendency to take flight from difficult situations; (b) her difficulty in anticipation and planning; and (c) her difficulty in understanding the effects of her behaviour on the children and how they felt confused by her. In addition, there was a sadistic quality to this denial of their needs and of her own authority as a parent. It was also noticeable that Mrs B had great difficulty in keeping the children in mind when they were not in her presence.

The psychotherapy sessions were also particularly difficult, as she tended to see interpretations and understanding as merely an attack on her capacities, and the transference had an almost psychotic feel to it. Particularly distressing was the fact that as long as a programme for the baby's soiling took place in the hospital he was clean but, as soon as the family went home, Mrs B was unable to continue to follow the programme and he returned to soiling.

Thus, the family improved well in the hospital where a structure was provided, but Mrs B had great difficulty in taking the structure with her. Various attempts were made to understand this fact in psychodynamic terms, for example, by means of interpretation in terms of her splitting and of her defence against overwhelming anxiety, and considerable efforts were made to help the family deal with day-to-day issues. Surprisingly, though there was only quite limited success in the hospital, the family had improved considerably in their community when followed up some months later.

Example 3: The 'C' Family: Connecting and Playing Together

Mrs C, in her early twenties, and her son 'James', aged five, were referred in order to attempt to bring them together after a number of separations. Mrs C had been hospitalized following an overdose and had shown great difficulties in coping with her son; indeed, he had been put into care twice and was being fostered prior to admission.

Mrs C showed evidence of severe psychopathology, with marked schizoid features and a tendency to lapse into primary process thinking and action. For example, following her consultation, she shaved her head completely and mused about looking like a baby.

Mrs C came from a large family of mixed race; her father was described as very strict and used physical punishment to discipline the family, who were expected to be at his beck and call. Her mother was described as sacrificing her life for her children, and still behaved as if they were all babies. Mrs C was intelligent and did well at a good school, but married at the age of eighteen and this interrupted her education. Her husband walked out when she became pregnant and did not take part in their subsequent life. James was a bright child, but difficult to manage because of his behaviour difficulties; in particular he had a large vocabulary of abusive language, which he often used.

An important dynamic in the mother–son relationship seemed to be a faulty connection. This was illustrated not only by their difficulties in staying together before admission and Mrs C's incapacity to attend to James' needs, but also from birth when there was a difficulty in breast-feeding. The story was that Mrs C was apparently told that her nipples were not long enough, and the great difficulty that she had in trying to feed James was put down to this fact. She described how somehow James could never take the breast, and later on was not interested in taking food from her.

In psychotherapy sessions in the hospital with Mrs C there was also a great difficulty in the connecting up of therapist and Mrs C. There were long silences and the therapist had a countertransference feeling that she was being shown what it felt like not to be in touch with what was going on in Mrs C's inner world. Mrs C often spoke in disjointed unfinished sentences, especially when describing her angry feelings with James, and she often talked as if they were merged as one. She described the feeling that because she had James, she must not talk about herself, but she also realized that this was perpetuating her own mother's view of the world.

Initially, Mrs C was somewhat isolated in the hospital; she somehow missed being included in the community rota for washing up, breakfast duty and cooking. However, she worked efficiently in her work area, which was the children's playroom, and at childrens' tea, but it was difficult to share a task with her, and she gave people the feeling that she was simply 'going through the motions'. Her nurse felt that he had to do all the work in making contact with Mrs C as she brought nothing to him. James settled to some extent in the Day Unit, but could only be managed in a one-to-one setting and his abusive swearing made a constant impact, irritating both staff and other children. As admission proceeded, Mrs C found a useful niche for herself in community cooking, and seemed to derive a genuine sense of personal validity from this role. In addition, a major piece of work which facilitated Mrs C and James connecting up was done when her therapist and nurse met both Mrs C and James for regular play sessions for a few weeks, when Mrs C's capacity to play with James was encouraged and some limited interpretation of symbolic material was made. Individual psychotherapy was subsequently arranged for James who responded well and became less constricted in his play and less anxious.

There were many improvements in the relationship between Mrs C and James. Attention to both the psychodynamic meaning of the resentment about being a mother and a capable adult, and attention to the basic work of being a mother during the day, seemed fundamental to the changes that took place, enabling them to live together once more on a stable footing.

Example 4: The 'D' Family: Unsafe Family

This family consisted of mother and father in their thirties, a two-year-old boy and a six-month-old girl. The family was admitted because the baby was at risk from being battered, or at least from coming to some physical harm. Mrs D had had a quite serious depression following the premature birth of the baby girl. It had been a very traumatic time in which the baby was in an incubator for long periods and had a considerable amount of medical attention. Following this, the mother began to show clear signs of wanting to harm the baby, such as by tampering with its feeds and shaking it very severely. Although there seemed a reasonable attachment to the two-year-old boy by both parents, the girl was handled, in particular by the mother, with very little interest and attachment.

The two main issues initially and subsequently were, on the one hand, to provide a safe network in the hospital and outside, and, on the other, to provide a focus of work on the relationship between the parents and the children, and particularly the lack of attachment between mother and baby. In order to facilitate both these pieces of work, a considerable amount of attention was paid to the parents' own problems about dependency.

Both parents were educated and middle-class professionals. Unfortunately, both of them had suffered major losses in the recent past; the only living close relative was the maternal grandmother who was described as possessive and uninterested in helping her own children. Mrs D was herself the younger of two siblings.

We had to provide a constant focus of attention throughout the whole day, particularly for the mother and baby, which meant, for example, that initially she was not left unaccompanied at feeding times, although this subsequently was not necessary. Mrs D herself had a devouring quality to her, which made nothing appear to her as sufficient or good enough. She regurgitated acidly anything which she was offered; she described how qualified people in the helping professions seemed just to enjoy privileged positions because they had power; and she tended to stimulate in people rescuing fantasies of a helpless lost soul, but when anybody tried to help she tended to find it crushing and denigrating and hence had to reject it.

Mr D's own parents were felt by him as making him feel impotent and helpless; he felt he had an over-protective, all-giving but essentially devaluing mother and a distant father. Both Mr and Mrs D were denigrating of staff and therapy and of any feelings of dependency that they might have. They talked quite openly about how resentful they felt at having to be in the hospital. They made staff feel that there was something quite vicious and uncomfortable about them, and they also talked for a considerable amount of time about wishing to leave the hospital and so bring their treatment to a premature end.

We tried to foster, in a relatively non-persecuting way, their own sharing of what each of them observed and how they were able to use it together. We attempted to do this by providing a non-persecuting model of noticing and talking. It was discovered that one of the dynamics of the family was that taking notice of one thing seemed to imply ignoring something else; for example, Mr D felt he was dropped if notice was being paid to his wife's anxieties; while Mrs D felt like dropping the baby because if improvement was noticed, she feared that the family would be discharged.

The main focus of the work became more and more the parents' inability to focus on the problem of separation and loss, linked in particular to their weekends at home: they would constantly come back very late on a Sunday night, which meant that they were not able to have the Sunday meal with the other patients, and it also meant that on the Monday morning the two-year-old boy was difficult to handle, and became quite disruptive for a while.

Therapy was primarily individually based with both individual and therapist coming together for occasional marital meetings, and there were also occasional meetings of the whole family. The treatment was a success in that the situation of risk disappeared and the family were able to leave, feeling that they had got something constructive from their stay. The staff also felt that this was a success; however, the whole treatment had required considerable attention to almost every aspect of the work of the day, certainly for the first six months or so while the safety of the baby was in doubt. The treatment also necessitated the staff having to deal with considerable amounts of verbal attack from the parents. These attacks had to be metabolized and fed back in appropriate forms, and this required that the senior staff paid particular attention to looking after the therapists.

EVENTS IN THE HOSPITAL COMMUNITY

It has been pointed out that material occupying the hospital during the day is used for therapeutic purposes for individual patients and families; the following example is designed to illustrate this theme.

In the weekly whole hospital staff group on a Wednesday, the following themes arose:

It was early September, just after the summer break. It had been discovered recently that various consulting rooms had been broken into, which was quite an unusual occurrence at the hospital. There was talk of doors being left open and rooms being emptied or feeling empty. There was a query about whether or not confidential material had been seen. There was a feeling that this was one example of intrusions into private areas that perhaps were taking place in other areas of the hospital outside of the consulting rooms. There had been one or two major staff changes recently so that people were feeling that boundaries between members of staff were shifting and new boundaries were being made. In addition, there had been a recent increase of night-time disturbances in which the duty nurse had been put under considerable stress and had to do more work than is customary in order to help patients to be settled for the night.

In the staff group a specific family then became the focus of discussion. The 'E' family consisted of mother and father and baby aged nine months. This particular family had been admitted as an emergency following a domiciliary visit as the mother was in a severe state of post-natal depression and could no longer look after the baby.

They had a rather horrific history in that their first child was born severely brain damaged, probably related to a severe antenatal haemorrhage in the pregnancy. Although the doctors looking after this first child felt that it should be allowed to die as it was so severely damaged, Mr and Mrs E managed to keep the baby alive for some eight months by means of intensive nursing care in which they would take turns virtually twenty-four hours a day to keep it alive, for example, by constant sucking out of its air way. The baby finally died when Mr and Mrs E gave it back to the hospital for a week or so, so that they could have a rest. Just at this time, Mrs E conceived a new baby. She subsequently had great difficulty in attaching herself to it and could hardly differentiate the dead baby from her live baby. In addition, there was a severe marital relationship with constant rows and violence and severe obsessional, near-psychotic psychopathology in Mrs E.

Following the general themes in the staff group, it was then discovered that the 'E' family had become special patients: it was realized that they did not attend any of the daily work groups in which all patients participate with nurses looking after areas of the hospital. They had not been going home on weekends for many weeks, so that there had been absolutely no differentiation of boundaries between the week and the weekend. This was also most unusual, as it is an expectation that families go home for the weekend in order to maintain contact with their outside world, unless there is a reason for them not to do so, such as in an emergency, or to work on specific issues. The family was not on a community cooking rota; other patients had become fed up with doing everything for them; and, in addition, there were quite marked differences of opinion in the nurse and therapist of the patient, resulting in the therapist realizing that she should take up much more of the hostility towards her in the transference. It was realized by coupling the general themes of the group with this particular family, that there was something that one could learn about the family's psychopathology and how the hospital was (or perhaps was not) dealing with it. The empty rooms seemed to be related to the empty space in Mrs E in which there was no space for the new baby. Mr and Mrs E wished for special intensive care with no boundaries, for example, with no return home at the weekend. They also wished to remain in their own private world, which was against the expectations of living in a community. They felt that sharing their private world was an intrusion into their rigidly held private space rather than a chance to be able to share anxieties.

After this meeting, the staff from the Family Unit were able to take up much more vigorously what the family had been doing and what they had been avoiding until then.

The following example describes a number of typical general themes which arise in the Family Unit and become the focus of attention.

Towards the end of one particular week approaching the Christmas holidays, it had been noted by the hospital administrator, as well as some of the nursing staff, that a number of cigarette ends had been found around the hospital. The place was beginning to look quite untidy and there was doubt about whether or not these cigarette ends belonged to the patients, the staff or the group of electricians who were in the process of rewiring the hospital. This rewiring process had entailed knocking a number of large holes, probably at times rather unnecessarily, into the precious plaster so that the place was beginning to look most untidy. There was a general feeling that the fabric of the hospital had been interfered with in a damaging way. Members of staff, as well as patients, had mixed feelings about what was happening; some people felt that this was the price one had to pay for modernization and others felt that the whole job had been botched.

In general, in the patient group and various meetings throughout the hospital, there was a fear of latent madness getting out of hand and a wish for staff to take over responsibility. In addition, there was quite an angry defiant independence; for example, patients en masse were not returning for their Sunday supper. This resulted in the children making it difficult for the parents to put them to bed on Sunday night and they also became quite disruptive in the Monday morning playgroup. In addition, the parents' wish to be looked after seemed to become greater than their wish to be adults and parents for their children. There were general rather typical complaints that there were not enough staff or that the nurses were not available, and that staff had too-high expectations of what the patients were able to do.

However, it was generally felt by staff that a number of patients at this moment of time were avoiding issues in their own treatment. It was also discovered that there was an interference with the way that milk was being supplied: a number of bottles of milk had gone missing, and suddenly the Family Unit found itself without enough milk. It turned out that individuals were plundering the milk without letting anyone know. In addition, one mother – Mrs C in the previous example – had been taking off the cream from the milk and had been feeling quite guilty that no one had discovered this until that week.

These various themes and observations are, of course, complex and one cannot very easily link all the themes to particular individuals. However, the fact that the fabric of the hospital had been interfered with, as well as the fact that there was a coming break, obviously precipitated feelings of rage, helplessness and a wish to be looked after, by the patients as a whole. Such feelings in the hospital are interpreted to some extent on a group level and more generally on an individual therapy basis, while expectations are maintained that whatever parents' feelings about wanting to be looked after, they are still expected to maintain their authority as parents to their children. Any other attitude on the part of the staff would really be a perversion of their work and an inappropriate use of their resources. Mrs C's own particular plundering of the cream of the resources in terms of the bottles of milk was taken up quite vigorously in her individual therapy sessions with some success.

5 A COMPLETE CASE HISTORY

In order to give a full picture of a Cassel treatment, this chapter consists of a description of an ultimately successfully rehabilitated family from admission to discharge and follow-up. Reports made by different workers at the time will be used where appropriate, as well as the addition of comments on the treatment, in order to give a clear and vivid picture of the complicated processes that arise during a family admission. Even though a considerable number of observations and comments are presented here, they still only represent a selection of what took place.

BACKGROUND TO THE REFERRAL

The referral to the Cassel Hospital stemmed from psychological assessment the couple, Mr and Mrs A, agreed to by Dr Arnon Bentovim, Consultant Child Psychiatrist at Great Ormond Street Hospital. The couple's legal counsel pressed for their right for a chance to parent their second child, 'M', following the fostering panel and court's arrangements for the injured first child's future. The first child was adopted and their second child, fostered since birth, at two years of age, was likely to go for adoption too. Social services had grave doubts about the prognosis for change because of the secrecy and concealment for a very long time of the non-accidental nature of the injuries to the first baby. Fractures at four weeks and then an injury to the mouth and a further fracture had led to the baby's removal from the parents at seven weeks of age. The mother gave as the reason that the father's inexperience might have resulted in rough handling which accidentally caused fractures. Having secured a care order, the department initiated a rehabilitation of the child, aged seven months, with her parents, monitored on a six-day-a-week basis by visits to the home. Further fractures occurred, and bruising to the eye and sides of the face resulted in the child being definitively removed, aged fourteen months. The couple accepted counselling at a family centre, which they found a positive experience leading to their finding the confidence to agree to psychiatric assessment as a means of getting a chance with their second child, by then born and received into care. Following an assessment at the Maudsley, the assessment with Dr Bentovim gave rise to the first disclosures by the father. Dr Bentovim considered there was a slight possibility of success dependent on the parents' considerable commitment to working on their difficulties at the Cassel Hospital. Meanwhile, the father was prosecuted in a police case, which gave rise to the making of a three-year probation order.

Prior to assessment of the family, the local social services team was seen for a consultation to ascertain whether or not an assessment was appropriate. This is not a routine occurrence, but social services requested the meeting before they would agree to support admission. When, subsequently, the family was seen, it was decided that, despite the bad injuries to the older child, it would be worthwhile to see if we could rehabilitate the parents and M. First of all, Mr A had owned up to the injuries and showed some insight as to why he was violent; second, the mother was now aware of her husband's violence and was somewhat suspicious of him. In addition, M had a good relationship with her mother. Mother was able to play well with her and M was happy and trusting once they came into the consulting room. M cried a little at first when they were collected, and so the foster mother had to come to the interview initially, but as the girl soon settled the foster mother then left.

Father felt that the abuse was mainly his fault. He clearly had authority problems; his own father used to be strict with him and he found it difficult to voice his own feelings. He felt he was a 'mother's boy', but he was also belittled for his rather high-pitched voice, particularly by his father. Mother had a post-natal depression and was a somewhat unpredictable person. Her childhood was uneventful she said, until adolescence when she and her mother clashed. She said her mother was the authority in the family, while her father was placid. The parents admitted to communication problems between themselves and that Mrs A needed to build up trust with her husband again. They found the counselling they had had locally very useful in the last year and it had enabled them to talk about their feelings more.

We planned to admit the family following my assessment, to test out more fully the couple's capacities. A home visit was done prior to admission and following a planning meeting with social services. The (male) nurse involved in both these meetings wrote an evocative report, from which are taken some extracts.

HOME VISIT REPORT

Communication Prior to Visit

An extremely difficult and tense planning meeting took place
where social services workers stated their anxieties and reluctance over the placement. Since this time, I feel that the
workers involved have been directly obstructive in my preparations for the family's admission and, in fact, failed to
bring M along to the home visit (she has been in foster care
since birth), or inform me of their decision. Letters sent to
the workers and the family informing them of the home visit
and proposed admission date, claim not to have been received
by either of the respective parties. Thus, preparations
prior to the home visit have been characterized by splits
amongst workers involved in the case, breakdowns in communication and difficulties in making contact, which I feel are
very significant to the case.

Presentation

The family have a one-bedroomed first-floor flat situated on
a quiet suburban estate. It was difficult to find due to the
absence of a street sign and a barely discernable door
number; thus, making contact with the family felt difficult.
The flat was immaculately kept with apparently new furnish-
ings, the walls adorned with photographs from their wedding
day and of their two children. Mr A is a small, uncertain and
very anxious young man with a moustache and held stare, he
looked pale, tired and fragile. Mrs A, who seemed lively
and open, was slim with shoulder-length brown hair. M was
not present as social services failed to show up with her.

Attitude to Visitors

The couple seemed perplexed at our arrival and said that they
weren't expecting our visit and claimed not to have received
a letter from me informing them of my proposed visit (they
are not on the phone). This felt extremely uncomfortable. Mr
A had opened the door, invited us in then skipped off up the
stairs, calling for his wife in a rather anxious manner that
required her to take responsibility for welcoming us and en-
quiring as to the nature of our visit.

Once sitting, Mr A stated that he had come to a decision after much thought, and that he had decided not to come to the hospital after all, feeling that this tragedy and the ensuing fight to have his children had made him feel hopeless and in need of a fresh start. He felt that his daughter needed to be settled and felt that she should be adopted by *his* father, as is their first child.

There was a push for the visit not to take place and I could begin to feel dismissed and unwanted. I suggested that they may well have anxieties about having contact with their daughter and ourselves, but we could discuss these, and I maintained that the visit should go ahead.

Initially, I felt both parents treated us with much mistrust and suspicion and I gained a sense that they struggled to keep us in mind as people who might have the capacity to listen and care. Towards the end, however, it seemed clear that we had made some positive impression upon them and that they could listen and make use of some of the things put to them. We were not offered refreshment and, considering our three-hour journey, I wondered about their capacity to have needs in mind and anticipate.

Relationships/Interaction

Mr A seemed very dependent upon his wife and could appear very passive. Mrs A would respond to this by speaking on his behalf. I found him secretive, rigid and very controlled with Mrs A struggling to collude with this. It appeared clear how difficult they find it to talk directly to one another and we reflected on how things can become detached and dangerous when communication breaks down. They seemed to have some insight into this matter of relating. Though assertive in making his feelings about admission clear, Mr A was very withholding with Mrs A, opting to 'tell' in case we found out. I sensed that these aspects could make them feel very angry with one another, with both of them seeming unclear of boundaries. Obviously it was difficult to get a sense of their relations with their daughter but, from our discussion, I sensed great reluctance to take on parental responsibility and that contact with her felt dangerous due to uncertainty over angry feelings, and that by choosing not to be admitted they were, in fact, protecting her from them. We discussed this in a very useful way, and talked about how we work with families in helping them to keep things safe. I felt a strong wish for someone to make things safe. Their relating to outside agencies seemed very split.

History

Mrs A described a happy childhood, during which her relationship with her father was warm and that with her mother was 'up and down'; she described ambivalent feelings towards her. She offered that her mother suffered from post-natal depression. Mr A refused to describe his background, simply reiterating that he was 'tired of all this'.

They knew each other as children through family ties and started dating when Mrs A was sixteen. They have been married for five years. Soon after marriage, they decided they wanted children and were initially delighted when Mrs A became pregnant.

When their baby was four weeks old, Mr A inflicted injuries including a fractured femur, ankle and ribs caused by squeezing. At twelve weeks, their first child was taken into care. At five months rehabilitation was introduced with social services supervision. However, as progress was deemed to be made and supervision relaxed, the injuries began to reoccur and she was again taken into care. She is now adopted by the paternal grandparents. When Mrs A became pregnant again, it was decided that M be taken into foster care from birth. She has never lived with her parents, though frequent supervision takes place. Mrs A offered that Mr A was having difficulties with his own father at the time and that this had caused him great stress.

Despite the horrendous nature of these incidents, the couple tended to convey that their main trouble was an obstructive social services department and seemed worryingly out of touch with the damage caused to their children or their role in this.

Reaction to Description of Hospital Life

Both were anxious about the nature of psychotherapy and the functioning of the hospital in general. Both responded blandly to our description with Mr A simply stating that he had made up his mind not to come already and Mrs A stating that she had pretty much expected our portrayal of hospital life. Both expressed their struggles to share feelings and anticipated that this would be difficult. I sensed little motivation from the couple to want to address their difficulties.

Assessment and Prediction

I felt that this couple were extremely resistant to treatment and terrified about coming together: I sensed that this felt very threatening and dangerous for them. I gained little sense of their capacity to parent and I felt very worried by this. They struggled to communicate with one another. These factors together made the prospect of admission feel worrying. What felt hopeful was that these anxieties were very much out in the open and up for discussion and I feel our structures and emphasis on relationships could help the couple keep their child safe and support their capacity to do this. Things will feel most dangerous, I predict, when treatment proceeds and supervision relaxes and this will have to be very carefully monitored and planned.

I feel the couple are terrified of coming together and I have great doubts about their capacity even to arrive for admission.

There was little doubt that, despite meetings with Cassel staff, the social services department felt pushed into considering rehabilitation by the High Court. From the nursing report their doubts were really understandable, given the couple's ambivalence. However, following the nursing visit, the couple were keen on admission, which eventually took place once tight supervision arrangements were in hand. These arrangements are fairly typical of the admission of such families.

'A' FAMILY SUPERVISION ARRANGEMENTS WITHIN THE HOSPITAL

INITIALLY, PARENTS NOT TO BE ALONE WITH M.

- Mr and Mrs A cannot at present supervise each other. There will be a named patient contact at all times who will supervise and support Mr and Mrs A in the care of M.

- Where possible, Mr and Mrs A should be with M in public places.

- M will share a bedroom with other girls around her age. If she wakes at night, Mr or Mrs A will wake the patient night contact who has agreed to supervise them.

• M will be attending playgroups with a nurse and patients – both parents and single adults – while her parents attend meetings.

• M will be baby-sat by appropriate patients while her parents attend any meeting/session jointly.

• M will have twice-weekly nursed baths so that her physical state can be monitored.

SUPERVISION OUTSIDE THE HOSPITAL

Mr and Mrs A may only take M out with another responsible adult: (a) another patient following discussion with duty nurse; or (b) a nurse. They may go as far as the local shops on Ham Parade and down to the duck pond on Ham Common, that is, the immediate locality only, initially.

NOTE TO SOCIAL SERVICES
It would be our aim to gradually relax this supervision programme when we have a better idea of how Mr and Mrs A manage. We would, following further discussion with you, like to do this towards the end of the assessment period, if it is deemed appropriate. One example might be: the day contact could be dropped as a requirement while retaining a contact at night. Mr and Mrs A would ask the day contact for support (when needed), rather than him or her automatically being there.

In order to convey the results of the assessment of the family, the following extracts are taken from my report to the court.

As a result of our initial assessment on this family, we have come to the conclusion that it would be unsafe to pursue further rehabilitation of the couple with their child, due to the continuing risk of violence from Mr A. We have, however, decided to offer a further assessment for the mother and child on their own, about which we feel more optimistic.

When I first saw this family for an out-patient consultation following a separate meeting I had with the social services Department prior to the consultation, it was clear that there were enormous concerns about the risks for M, were she to remain with her parents. The reason for this was the severe injuries their first child was subjected to. At first, Mr A had not owned up to what had happened; however, he later did. It is not, of course, only the fact that he himself was responsible for the physical injuries, but that his wife appeared not to have noticed anything wrong or not to have reported it and this is of great concern. When I saw the three of them together, what struck me was that there was a clear bond between mother and child. It was as a result of this that I thought it was in M's interest to pursue an assessment at the Cassel to look at the various possibilities.

I shall now go through each parent and the child in turn, looking at our findings and then summarize the overall picture.

M was seen four times by one of our child psychothera-pists, twice with both her parents and then twice with her mother alone. Her parents were also both seen before M's arrival in order to think about the difficulties that she may have in settling. From the beginning, M struck the therapist as an unusually self-possessed little girl. Her development seems good, she is curious and interested in toys and plays with concentration and enjoyment with the dolls, and so on. She often talks to herself while she is doing this although, as yet, her speech is difficult to understand, unless she is directly asking for something. She settled into the hospital reasonably well. There were times when M showed a degree of self-reliance and distance, not wanting any help and wanting things her own way. Her mother found this quite difficult. Significantly, in relation to the therapist, M showed no curiosity and little eye contact; she was eager to try the toys, but she did not relate to the therapist as a person. When the therapist mentioned this to Mrs A, she described how, on access visits, M often seemed to be more interested in the toys or sweets they brought, than greeting them. This made us wonder how much M has been able to develop the capacity for real attachment, given the uncertainty of her placement plans and her experiences of her parents as inter-mittent visitors in her life. This makes it imperative that a permanent decision about her future is made as soon as possible. Hence the need for a further full assessment of mother's capabilities. It is difficult, at this stage, to gain a clear picture of M's needs, due to the uncertainties in her life. However, it does seem that M will need help to develop close dependent relationships and that should we continue a further assessment, her mother's ability to become sensitive to her needs will be a crucial issue in the assessment of M's future placement.

This was a threatening admission for Mr A and he has been an anxious and defensive patient to get to know. He has had weekly individual sessions, plus twice-weekly group sessions, as well as marital sessions with his wife. He reacted to the hospital with a well-meaning intent that we felt was unreal. He appeared empty of any capacity to be in conflict, straining to present himself as totally cooperative and attuned to what was expected of him. He came across, in fact, as rather cool, lacking in feeling and deep emotion, and gave a rather trivial account of the horrendous injuries to his first child. In sessions, he emphasized his loss of a protecting father in his own life. Mr A was generally experienced as a rather shallow and anxious man. He has experienced severe humiliation at the hands of his parents. He described his relationship with his mother as being over-close, and describes as a child being 'tied to her apron strings'. He feels that his mother was extremely cruel and sadistic towards him and he hates her for this. He describes feeling unwanted by his father, who would have preferred a girl instead. Mr A felt that his father was contemptuous and mocking of him and he experienced this as an attack on his masculinity. He was persecuted by bullying at school, and his parents divorced in his late teens.

Mr A is controlling and possessive of his wife; both are terrified of angry feelings and both are extremely dependent, yet hate and feel contempt towards dependency. Mr A struggles to share his wife with other people and can feel envious, jealous and enraged by this. On the whole, we found him rather cut off and emotionless. Although there were no obvious incidents of violence in the hospital we nonetheless felt very anxious indeed about Mr A's capacity for violence. We found him chilling and frightening, at times, in the way he talked about the past abuse and the way that he tends to gloss over his own impulses. We felt sympathetic towards the fact that he had been humiliated as a child and that there was obviously a depth of despair and hopelessness in him. We felt strongly that he needed treatment in his own right, but we also felt he was not yet ready to be a safe parent. We felt that his capacity to control himself was fairly tenuous and I would certainly not be prepared to take a risk, either as an out-patient or an in-patient, with continuing rehabilitation with him involved in the family.

Mrs A has a tendency to withdraw behind the facade where everything seems all right and happy. She comes across as a dependent person who would like to put the responsibility onto others. We, so far, have a rather vague, sketchy picture of her background. She describes her relationship with her father as warm and loving and describes ambivalence towards her mother. Her teenage years were marked by rebellion and heated rows with her mother. She also describes her father as being on her side, but rather weak and not being able to stand up to her, and mother as very controlling and demanding, expecting her daughter either to stay at home and obey her or to leave for good.

Although she would like to think of herself as someone who is independent and seems to have projected all the dependency on to her husband for some time, her own dependency need seems so strong that she needs someone else to feel complete. The danger of this situation is that she then sees in this other person only what she projects into him or her and this possibly is one of the reasons why she couldn't see anything other than a happy father in her husband until he admitted responsibility for their child's injuries. Mrs A also has difficulty staying with ambivalent feelings of love and hatred and tends to split them and project them into different people. This seems to have enabled her to have a very close relationship with her husband so long as they could fight social services. However, this shifted dramatically when the child came to stay with them in the hospital and she then became the object of her love and her husband then became the object of anger, frustration and hatred.

There is definite love and affection for her child and she is able to be in touch with her and play with her but, at the same time, one wonders how much she needs the child to look after her. As so much of Mrs A's preoccupations have been with her husband, it is difficult to know at this point what will happen in the further period of assessment. We will certainly get a much more realistic view of her mothering capacities. Up to now, Mrs A has certainly been the prominent parent figure in the care of M, with Mr A's role seeming a more subsidiary one; indeed, at times remote. We have noticed a warm and affectionate bond between M and her mother – she actively shares with her and seeks her out and turns to her in times of distress for help and support. At the same time, M can control and dominate her parents in an omnipotent way, which has made them feel uneasy and they can feel paralysed by her. This is probably a response to the parents' own doubts at the time of the assessment about whether or not they were going to stay.

As the assessment proceeded, Mrs A became more and more clear that she did not want to be with her husband and that she felt it would be more realistic to see if she could be rehabilitated with her daughter. I think this wish should be respected in the first place. The doubts, of course, are first of all to continue the uncertainty for M. However, she has settled well into the hospital and has not shown obvious

signs of distress coming in and being with her mother. The
other main doubt is whether the mother would seriously separate from her husband or whether this is just a temporary
phase. My feeling, at the moment, is that I think she is
quite serious but this may well have to be tested. For the
new assessment to proceed, it would have to be clear that the
father would leave the matrimonial home, otherwise I can
foresee a dangerous situation with the mother being
rehabilitated with the child possibly and then going home to
a potentially violent relationship.

In summary, we recommend that a further period of assessment be offered for mother and child. The main reasons for
not accepting the father are his immaturity, his history of
severe sadistic violence to his first child and his lack of
in-touchness with his violence, and we have overwhelming
feelings of anxiety about what might happen with his second
child. He also says that everything is all right when clearly
it is not, and there is a denial of the problems. However, we
do feel that he would need and benefit from treatment in his
own right somewhere else. Away from her husband, Mrs A may be
able to look more effectively at mothering issues. She has
been intimidated by her husband and certainly been preoccupied by him. Our concern is her lack of awareness of what had
been going on before and her tendency to cut off from her
emotions. Nonetheless, she does have a good bond with her
child and I feel it would be quite wrong not to give her one
last chance.

As a result of our recommendations, mother and daughter remained
in the unit for a further period of assessment. The supervision
arrangements were reduced and soon removed, as it was not felt that
there was much actual physical danger to her daughter. Individual
and small group therapy continued for mother, while a child psychotherapist continued to see mother and daughter together. At the next
assessment, there were still major concerns about mother's lack of
emotional engagement with staff and with her daughter, yet there
were enough positive features to indicate that rehabilitation should
proceed, as can be seen in the following extracts from the relevant
reports.

SECOND NURSING ASSESSMENT OF THE 'A' FAMILY

This has been the second period of assessment. It felt important for us to examine more closely the mother–child relationship following the discharge of Mr A, prior to the directions hearing. Mr A's departure initially left Mrs A with a great sense of relief which allowed her to engage rather automatically more closely in her relationships, both within the hospital and outside. I feel it is significant that she has regained contact with her parents after some considerable time. The absence of her turbulent relationship with her husband has also allowed her to focus more clearly on her relationship with M and I feel she has been more able to both anticipate and meet her daughter's needs. This, in my opinion has led to a strengthening of the bonding between them.

The air of hopefulness and relief brought about by Mr A's departure has, however, given way to feelings of despair which have been available for work in the nursing area. Along with Mr A, I think she has attempted to rid and deny her own difficulties and those that her husband has emulated, hence her own anger and violent feelings; her sense of denigration and humiliation.

I feel Mrs A is more aware of her aggressive feelings and her passive destructiveness. She is terrified of angry feelings and tends to switch off from them.

She is aware of how M can make her feel useless at times; for example, when she fails to comfort her fears, or fails in her discipline and sanctioning. Mrs A is extremely shy and inhibited and I think can be envious of her daughter's gregarious, spontaneous and lively interactions with others. Mrs A therefore struggles both with the anger and sense of uselessness that can be stirred up in the relationship with her daughter.

There seem to be two clear aspects of Mrs A's relating. On the one hand, she can be lively and engaged with M and at these times one senses affection between them. This allows M to be lively and free to explore her relationships and world. On the other hand, at other times Mrs A is flat, inert and deadening, which detrimentally affects her relationship with her daughter who also, at these times, can become anxious and fearful and more clingy. Underneath the surface, I think Mrs A is extremely depressed. She can feel hopeless and despairing over her own upbringing and therefore in her own parenting capacities and feelings towards children.

I feel M is generally more settled. She has been able to be

more separate from her mother - initially there was a tendency for them to cling together - and free to explore relationships beyond her mother. She plays freely with the other children in the nursery and has formed close relationships with some of the adults and children within the hospital. I feel she has more confidence in her mother's capacity to provide care generally. Bath times, meal times and bed times proceed more fluently. She is deeply attuned to her mother's feelings and picks up her mother's despair and becomes anxious and tearful at these times. It has been a period of illness for her, which I feel expresses some of her vulnerability. Mrs A has been able to respond well and comfort M, giving her the appropriate care at such times. M has more recently been aware of loss. This followed her weekend stay at the hospital, in which she was aware of the absence of her foster mother and her father. She is preoccupied with this sense of loss at present. There was a period of accident-proneness which I feel is directly related to her preoccupation with loss, and also to tiredness when her routine of an afternoon nap is neglected. Her weekends with her foster mother have also been more settled and although M misses her at times and is aware of her absence, she is able to keep her in mind and has some degree of object constancy.

Separation and loss seem to be important areas for them both. Mrs A responded to my absence with initial rage which quickly gave way to a sense of abandonment, disillusionment and despair. She finds M's absence at weekends very painful; this makes hand-overs awkward at times.

In conclusion, I feel there is a greater affinity between mother and daughter which reflects some of the positive aspects of the mother's relationship. I feel this is hopeful and on these grounds a period of treatment and rehabilitation could be most beneficial. However, I feel cautious as there are many areas of difficulty and Mrs A requires sustained help and support in her mothering; I have some sense of her being able to use this. It would seem critical to engage in treatment both the aggressive and depressive natures of her personality and these seem difficult to reach at times. Mrs A can be secretive and collusive in her relationships; she still has a tendency to be withdrawn and isolated and struggles to participate in group orientated activities.

Some areas of nursing work would include:

1. Mrs A's capacity to play and interact verbally with her daughter will require sustained work and would be a major focus, that is, supervised playgroups.

2. The need for Mrs A to take on more responsibility, that is, jobs in the hospital, which also demand working along-side others.

3. The exploring of angry and sad feelings in relation to separation and loss. This can usefully be explored in the context of weekends.
4. Continued examination and anticipation of M's needs and how these can be met.

INDIVIDUAL PSYCHOTHERAPIST'S SECOND ASSESSMENT REPORT RE MRS A

Since the first review on family A, Mrs A has been attending her sessions regularly and always on time, except that she had to miss two sessions because of my own sickness. After the review and when Mr A had left, she felt quite relieved and she appeared to be livelier and more open. As I under-stood it, she seemed to be relieved about the separation for two reasons. On the one hand, I think she had felt very tense and very unhappy in the relationship, at least recently, so she felt that by separating she did the right thing and that this gave a new opportunity to her life and the relationship with M. On the other hand, there seemed to be a more patho-logical relief, because she seemed to have put all the re-sponsibility, blame, destructiveness and guilt for it into him and felt that by separating from that externally, she could resolve the situation internally. This led to a fear of anything of that nature being brought up. Thus, for example, she was very afraid of talking to M about Daddy because of the fear that M would then just be 'going on and on and on' about Daddy, and she seemed very reluctant to think in any way about him and her relationship to him and her own part in that. I got the impression that she just wanted to wipe out any memory of him, just as she cut him off a picture of the three of them on the first occasion they went out, so that it left her with a picture of just her and her daughter. This wish to wipe out not only Mr A but other things that troubled her made her at times quite inhibited in the session where I felt she wanted to avoid, at all costs, getting into these areas.

On the other hand, she appeared more flexible in her mind and more open and lively than she had before. While she had been primarily focused on her hatred of Mr A in the sessions before the review, she was now able to experience different kinds of feelings (sadness about what had happened, feelings of guilt about it, love for M, fear of criticism, and so on) and was able to explore different areas of her present and past life. With M being here on a more permanent basis she was able to get more in touch with her feelings of love towards her. She talked about the deep bond she had felt after birth and in hospital, and how she later had to bottle that up and save it for the few access visits and how very painful she felt it was to wait for so long, to see her for just a little while and then have to leave again. Having got into contact with M again and with her own attachment to her, it was difficult and sometimes impossible for her to keep in mind that she was still in care and that there was still a foster mother there to have her on the weekends. Some of the difficulties of the hand-over seem to be that she tried to push aside any thoughts and feelings about that until the last moment when the hand-over was due, and then she got into a mixture of anger and despair. I think that in the sessions I could see, at times, a mother who was able to love her child and think of her and care for her, but I could also see a mother who was so dependent on the child that she couldn't separate from her and couldn't easily think about her needs. It was, at least partly, that which made it impossible for her to see when her first child was being injured again; that Mrs A was so afraid of losing her that she turned a blind eye to what she saw and thus failed to protect her. I think that this is one of the worrying states she can get into where she is so absorbed by her own feelings that she cannot see what is going on outside of her. On the other hand, I do feel that this is something she is able to work on.

Mrs A reacted very strongly to her nurse's absence when he was working in the community team for a couple of weeks. She seemed to miss him very much, but then in her mind he seemed to become the only person she could get help from and no one else seemed available for her or good enough. Her frustration and anger led her to withdraw into a kind of encapsulated state out of which she couldn't make contact – for example, couldn't go up to him and talk to him – and in some state of projection, she felt that he was totally disinterested in her. Something of the same sort I think happened later, when I was off sick for a week, because when I came back she was very withdrawn and it wasn't until the second session after coming back that she was able to make some contact with me again. This, again, I think is one of the more worrying states Mrs A can get into, where she is absorbed with herself and her own feelings and projections and cannot get in touch with other people again and make contact with them and take back some of the projections. I suspect that she can pull M into these states as someone she can cling to. On the other hand, I feel that with our being aware of that, she can be helped to get out of these states again, and in a longer period of therapy, could be helped to work these things through.

While Mrs A, in the beginning, seemed to deny any uncertainty about her mothering capacity, she was then later able to express her insecurity and to think about it, and I got the impression that by doing so she has actually developed and increased her mothering capacity. I also feel that she felt some gratitude for what she gets here, which was, for example, expressed in a thought that she should have had something like this in the beginning with her first child.

I think that there are still major areas within her that need to be worked on and yet haven't really appeared in her therapy. Particularly, her own aggressive side would have appeared more as persecutory feelings than as her own aggression.

In the second assessment, it was also reported that M, who was by then just over two years old, had moved from a self-reliant, unrelating stance to a more related way of interacting. She remembered toys in the therapy room and played with them and, in general, seemed happier. In the nursery, she played age-appropriately, but mainly going her own way. In groups, mother said very little and there was a sense of her not really being engaged. There were also housing difficulties, as mother had given up her tenancy to her husband, which she had done without consulting with staff.

There was general agreement to recommend rehabilitation. The focus of work was to be:

1. The mother–child relationship – looking at play, and exploring ambivalent feelings.

2. The need for mother to take more responsibility for herself – housing needed to be sorted out; she could take on a job in the community, such as children's supper manager.

3. The overall issue of mother's need to become more of an individual, as well as her fear of emotional closeness.

Although rehabilitation was recommended and apparently agreed to by social services, in fact it was a year before it began. This was partly as a result of the delay in finding a suitable flat for mother and daughter; partly because of the ambivalence about rehabilitation from social services; and partly because of mother's own difficulty in convincing them of her mothering capacity. On the one hand, the delay was unfortunate, as M's future continued to be uncertain; on the other hand, it did allow mother more time to develop as a person. However, mother became so angry with social services' delay in facilitating rehabilitation that at one time she began another destructive relationship with a man. Although fleeting relationships may occur at times when parents are waiting for rehabilitation, this relationship for a time seemed to put the whole treatment in doubt. Further extracts from review reports indicate the situation at that time.

'A' FAMILY REVIEW

At the last review, we had an overall sense of both Mrs A and her daughter developing. We recommended that it was appropriate now for her rehabilitation process to continue. Since this period, treatment seems to have come to a standstill.

Extensive rehabilitation plans were drawn up, however, at a Child Care Review, and some useful amendments were suggested by the social services department. They also advised us that, for statutory reasons, the process could not commence until all the child placement regulations had been fulfilled. Mrs A's response to this was very dramatic. What followed was a period of despair and hopelessness that she would ever be reunited with her daughter. This was followed by a very destructive rage towards social services and the hospital, whom she saw as restricting her progress. Although this reaction in part seemed appropriate, it also seemed unrealistically excessive and since then I feel has been used defensively as a way of avoiding thinking about some of the difficulties, fears and uncertainties that going home with M would mean. This period of despair and rage was then exacerbated following the announcement that her workers at the Cassel Hospital would either be leaving or changing units. Since then, I feel Mrs A has felt quite uncontained and mindless. Although her care of M can be excellent, this period has shown how desperately she can struggle to have her daughter in her mind when she feels so neglected, abandoned and angry herself.

Mrs A has found it unbearable being at the hospital. Her relationships here with other adults are appalling. I feel she has disengaged and become more isolated and I feel this is worrying. This has coincided with a period of suspicion and rumour that Mrs A was having a relationship with X. It has since become clear that this is the case. I feel Mrs A has been quite cut off from both the fears and the anxieties that going home with M would instil in her. Additionally, I am concerned about her disturbed relationships and particularly those formed with men. In a sense, it has been me who has raised these concerns whilst she has been quite oblivious to them, but I felt that underneath she also is quite disturbed by both the doubts and the negative feelings she can have about mothering and towards her daughter. I feel she is quite disturbed about why it is so difficult for her to form ordinary relationships and why she persistently forms destructive relationships with men. In a way, these disturbances have become available in the treatment but Mrs A paradoxically has not been. Mrs A clearly loves her daughter and is able to provide for her. It would be wrong to suggest that M is thriving, but she is extremely fond of her mother and can feel cared for and looked after adequately. However, there can remain a worrying distance between them when feelings of distress are around, particularly the more depressed and chaotic feelings within Mrs A, and these, I feel, lead us to a clue as to why this distance persists. I feel this is a crucial period in this family's treatment. I feel we need to help Mrs A face both her negative feelings towards her daughter and her role as a parent. I feel we also need to help her face the reality of her relationships and to work on ways in which these can be improved or mended. I feel a period of being settled in treatment is now necessary. However, to slow the rehabilitation process up for much longer would be disastrous and I believe it would lead to the breakdown of this family and be an unnecessary obstacle to their progress. Mrs A has found it almost unbearable to face the leaving of her various workers. Mrs A is terrified of her dependency on others. I feel this gets in the way of her forming anything beyond superficial relationships but also means that she doesn't have to face the pain of loss which she clearly is experiencing in relation to her workers.

Nursing aims should be as follows:

1. First and foremost, her relationships within the community. This needs to be explored through high-profile jobs such as the pantry or the community chairperson.

2. Exploring this distance that can be present between her and her daughter, what this represents and ways of working with this.

3. I feel Mrs A needs the confidence of a course; of contact in the outside world, as well as within the hospital.

INDIVIDUAL PSYCHOTHERAPIST'S REPORT ON MRS A

I have been seeing Mrs A in individual therapy twice a week for a year.

Generally, I feel that Mrs A has moved on considerably and has been able to use her individual treatment as a whole, although or maybe because there have been quite difficult times with her, I feel that I as her individual therapist, the child psychotherapist and her nurse, have gone through great struggles with her. Although she can sometimes dismiss that or feel so frustrated that she just wants to give up, and although she has felt angry that all her workers are moving, I think she is basically aware of having gained a lot here and is grateful for that.

Mrs A has become much more of a 'person', someone who appears alive with all sorts of feelings, whereas in the beginning she appeared very flat, stiff, rigid and imprisoned. She had a very imprisoned relationship with her husband in which they tried to be very harmonious and all the aggressiveness was apparently projected outwards. But she also was very imprisoned in herself and had enormous difficulties showing and speaking about any kind of inner feelings. One reason for that was a very persecuted state of mind where she was always expecting criticisms and attacks and was extremely guarded. She was extremely inhibited with her own aggressive feelings and had a sense of a very strong and harsh super-ego which attacked and criticized her all the time. This has changed considerably, and although these features are of course still around, Mrs A has been able to reach a point where she feels more confident about herself and less criticized and attacked, and where she can deal much more with her own anger and aggression and doesn't have to project these feelings outwards so much. On the other hand, it remains an issue that any firmness, any healthy aggressiveness, can be experienced by her as something unbearably aggressive and that has been a problem in dealing with her daughter, particularly since M has been much more aggressive and provocative herself.

Mrs A had a great potential to withdraw into 'encapsulated states'. These were states in which she would be so preoccupied with her own worries, projections and wishes that she would not be able to take in what the other person said or think about the other person. These states often seemed quite worrying when thinking about her ability to care for a child, and her inability to protect her first child from being injured by her husband, I think, was partly due to such states. I remember a family meeting with Mrs A in May when she felt she was sitting with three judges, and that made her completely unable to respond to M. At one point, she just ran out of the meeting. It can be particularly difficult for Mrs A to ask for any help if she is distressed and worried; partly because she is afraid of being criticized and attacked rather than helped. We had some times during her treatment where she would retreat completely and be inaccessible to me in her sessions and to others in other settings, and where it was only possible much later to speak about the state of despair and worry she had been in. Again, I think this propensity to retreat into an encapsulated state has lessened considerably and she has been much more able to be open about herself and ask for help, and certainly she has been much more able to respond to M and avoid withdrawing from her completely. Nevertheless, I would say it remains a feature of her.

It has been difficult to think with Mrs A about her role in the first child's injuries. For a long time that was impossible, because she felt accused of having inflicted the injuries herself, if anything was brought up. One important reason on her part was certainly, as stated earlier, her propensity to get so caught up with herself, her worries and her projections that she was unable to reach out, which made her unable to protect the child. Another reason, I think, was a projection or delegation of something violent in herself, and this has been much more difficult to work on. Only when she had been in a relationship for one or two months with a man who appeared to her, in many ways, like her husband did she start to think about what made her choose such a man. She was struck that this man, like Mr A, appeared soft and dependent, but was talking about violent accidents and memories. I don't think that we got very far in thinking about that, but she was worried by it so much that she stopped that relationship.

An important issue in her treatment has been her deep dependency and her massive defences against that. Whilst she was with her husband, who was a very dependent person, he showed so much dependency that she could experience him as the dependent one and herself as the independent one. She was surprised when she had another, brief, relationship to find herself again with a very dependent person who also hadn't been able to separate from his mother. It is striking that she thought of herself as being very independent as an adolescent, but then before she left home, started the relationship with

Mr A, who had been the child of neighbours. During long periods of her treatment, she thought of herself as very independent, but was quite furious at times, with her nurse in particular, when she felt she wasn't looked after properly and not enough time was given to her. For a long time in the summer, she came back from weekends being very dismissive of the hospital and feeling that she didn't want to come back. Although there were other reasons, this was certainly also linked with her defence against feeling dependent on the hospital. When she had a week off at the beginning of the summer, she had in some way thought of that as enjoying her freedom and independence, but then before leaving she felt quite worried and almost pushed out by us. When actually on her own, she experienced quite a depression and despair. However, at that time, she was able to stick with it and not to take flight from it. For some time, I think, she tried to draw M into a state of strong mutual dependency and she seemed to wish to be with her in a close twosome separated from the rest of the world as she had been with her husband. Both her own and M's development has allowed them to be more separate and independent in the meantime. For some time, Mrs A was in a highly eroticized transference relationship with her male nurse and it was very difficult during that period to work in any way on that and to think about it, but I think it was part of her defence against her dependency and against her rage about being separate and left alone.

In the beginning, Mrs A had thought about herself as having no problems and not being in need of any treatment. However, she has come to realize her difficulties. It has been a problem that the social services department has not been able to recognize sufficiently the shift she has made, both in acknowledging her own problems and in working on and changing them. Therefore, she experienced a lot of frustration and had to put up with having to wait a long time for anything to move on. The resistant attitude of social services has often made it more difficult in the treatment, because they were seen as the obstructors and behaved as such, and she could be upset about it or fight against it. That often made it more difficult for her to think about her own worries and ambivalences and about good reasons to wait rather than rush into rehabilitation too quickly. The latest decision of social services to stop the continuation of rehabilitation until all the parties asked have given their opinions, led to a deep feeling of frustration, anger and hopelessness and sometimes she felt like giving up. The fact that her nurse announced his leaving the Unit has added to that, because she has felt quite supported by him and he has been battling with social services on her behalf.

Apart from her strong transference love towards her nurse, she has also developed an eroticized relationship towards me, but that has been quite difficult to address, because it has always been more hidden and expressed only in her somewhat shy and nervous smile. So in some way, it has been more in the air than really worked on. She has found it quite difficult to accept my leaving and has shifted between anger, hopelessness, feeling cut-off and sadness.

The child psychotherapist who was seeing mother and daughter left on maternity leave, which was obviously another powerful factor which affected mother. The therapist wrote a transfer summary for a new therapist.

FROM TRANSFER SUMMARY

I have seen Mrs A and M once-weekly for a year since their admission. During the assessment, I was struck by the emotional distance between M and her parents. M seemed a lively, interested girl, whose development was good, but there was awkwardness between her and her parents. She played with her back to them both, apparently absorbed in her own game, not wanting or needing to interact with them. Although I was aware that M had been living separately from her parents, I felt this did not explain entirely the distance in their relationship, considering that they had frequent access.

In the following months of work with M and her mother, I realized that this initial impression of emotional distance and awkwardness was due to Mrs A's difficulty in developing a close responsive relationship to her daughter. She was so frozen in exploring her own feelings of distress and anger that she found it impossible to respond to these feelings in M, who was confused and disturbed by the many experiences of loss she had been through. First, she had been separated from her mother, then her foster father who died, then her foster mother who she now saw only at weekends, and now recently her father who left treatment. Mrs A felt embarrassed in the mother-child sessions, not able to cope with the idea of playing with her child in front of me as an observer and quick to see my comments as criticism of her mothering, rather than a support to it.

In contrast, it soon became clear that M could relate closely and warmly, given the opportunity. Her development continued to progress well, her speech became clearer and her exploration and use of the toys became more imaginative and detailed. She enjoyed and looked forward to her sessions and used them to show us in play the particular issues that were worrying her or preoccupying her. Typically, these related to her upset and anger about her mother leaving her at weekends with her foster mother and her anger about the long break over Christmas. Also, she showed us her confusion about her father leaving and the loss of her 'uncle' (that is, her foster father). The focus of my work was often in helping Mrs A find the words to talk to M about these events, so that she could be helped to understand what had happened and why, and also, to help mother give M the comfort and closeness she needed when talking about some painful issues. Mrs A gradually became more comfortable with me and was able to acknowledge a need for help in this area.

Over time, Mrs A has become more spontaneous and intimate in her relationship with M and more open in managing the feelings of anger and sadness in their relationship. M has also become more assertive and challenging of her mother and Mrs A has needed help to be firm and say no. She has worried about losing her temper with M, for example, over bed time routines, and has been able to talk about how she could handle these more appropriately. Alongside this focus on difficult areas, there have been many occasions when I have simply enjoyed observing M and Mrs A playing together and commented on the good quality of care that mother has been able to offer. The difficulties occur when Mrs A is tense or angry and goes into her shell. At these times, she appears to lose the skills she has gained in relating to her daughter and needs considerable help to overcome her resistance and relate once more to M, who is less rejected and confused by this response from her mother.

Recent Events

It is difficult to know what has caused the recent crisis in treatment with Mrs A, who first refused to work and then left the hospital, apparently in defiance of the Cassel Hospital and social services. I was not sure how much this was due to external factors like a new relationship with X, or the delays in social services' agreement to her rehabilitation, or her ambivalence to taking on full care of M once rehabilitation was a real prospect. The added dimension of the loss of her treatment team – her nurse, her therapist, and myself due to maternity leave – which has brought to the surface again her difficulties in dealing with feelings of separation,

loss and anger, was clearly an added stress. She has now
finally returned to the hospital and I hope it will be possible to recommence treatment to clarify these issues and
also to finish my work with M and her mother, and say goodbye.

Conclusion

M and her mother have developed a good relationship while at
the Cassel. M has been developing well and her mother has
shown potential for good mothering. However, Mrs A's difficulties in social relationships, her difficulty in dealing
with conflict and resolving her ambivalence about taking on
M's care, are issues which still need to be worked with and
clarified in treatment. In terms of mother-child work, the
focus would need to continue on looking at mother's ability
to deal with both positive and negative aspects in her
relationship with M and to be responsive to her child's
needs. It will also be important for her to discover that she
can transfer what we have worked on together into a new relationship with a child therapist in preparation for taking
the skills she has learned at the hospital back into the
community.

In the end, faced by the choice between X and her daughter,
Mrs A chose the latter and was able to separate from X. The
episode with him seemed to be very much related to her sense
of loss of the Cassel workers, in addition to her frustrations over
the delays in rehabilitation. Despite his obvious major problems,
X seemed to offer a solution, a way out of her difficulties. However, she was able to put her child first, and she eventually
managed to proceed with rehabilitation, which finally began one
year following the initial recommendation and with a completely
new set of Cassel workers. Only limited work looking at inter-
agency issues was possible with social services, who tended to
retain a rather rigid position.

A graded rehabilitation plan was drawn up, to enable M
gradually to say goodbye to her foster mother and for mother
and daughter gradually to go to mother's new home. The following outline gives some of the details of this plan.

REHABILITATION PLAN: FIRST STAGE: MRS A AND M

29 November	Home visit accompanied by nurse.
15 December	Day visit home, mother and daughter.
30 December	Mrs A and M to spend day together. M returns to foster carers at 6 p.m. Social services to visit.
3 January	Mrs A and M day together. Unplanned visit social services. Return to Cassel late afternoon.
5 January	Meeting at the Cassel with social services department to discuss rehabilitation so far. Child care planning meeting 1 February. Recommendation for further rehabilitation.
Christmas	Mother and M at Cassel until 28 December. M goes to foster mother on 28 December. Mrs A home. Return to Cassel on 3 January, approximately 5 p.m.
10 January	First overnight stay. Return 1.30–2.00 p.m. Wednesday.
Weeks ending:	
13–15 January	M two nights with foster mother. Mrs A to see first child.
20–22 January	Second overnight stay. Leave after lunch Friday. Return 6 p.m. Saturday.
27–29 January	Third overnight stay. Leave after lunch Friday. M to foster mother 12 midday on Saturday. Return to hospital on Sunday p.m.
3 February	Fourth overnight stay. M to foster mother Saturday 12 midday to Sunday p.m. Return to Cassel Sunday p.m. Child care planning meeting 8 February (social services). Review at Cassel 9 February.
10 February	Possible first weekend stay.

The new nurse's description of mother and daughter's first visit home included the following.

FIRST HOME VISIT 29 NOVEMBER: MRS A AND M

Beginning of Rehabilitation

M appeared to be very excited about the prospect of going to 'Mummy's house' and asked Mrs A lots of questions regarding the house. It was obvious that Mrs A had prepared M for the visit by telling her about the Christmas tree and various toys which she could play with. M had not visited her mother's home for more than a year.

The journey took four hours and Mrs A had found it difficult to plan the route, so we went by the longest route. She appeared anxious about sorting this out on Monday, perhaps because of the short notice that the visit was going ahead and the number of arrangements which had to be made on her return to the hospital on Monday lunchtime.

M was quite demanding during the train journey and Mrs A found it difficult to set limits with her; for example, she demanded food very early on in the journey, but was not happy with the various food options with which Mrs A presented her, and continued to scream and cry. Mrs A had to remove her from the pushchair and managed to distract her by looking at a book and giving cuddles. M responded to this.

The house was very clean and very nicely decorated. It was obvious that Mrs A had spent a lot of time preparing for M's visit and that it meant a lot to her.

M explored the sitting room and wanted to touch and remove ornaments from the mantelpiece. She remembered one of these ornaments from her last visit. She appeared fascinated by the Christmas tree and returned to it on a number of occasions, having left it to explore another area/room in the house. She was keen to go back into her bedroom on a number of occasions. Mrs A had decorated the bedroom in a very child-centred way, with a colourful quilt cover, dolls and teddy bears on the bed.

Mrs A appeared anxious as to what to do at first but, as soon as I encouraged her to spend time playing with M, she got down on the floor and engaged with M very appropriately. She went to the bedroom on M's request and played with her there.

Mrs A responded to M's request to look through some photographs and M saw photos of her sister, who she perceived as herself. Mrs A explained who her sister was.

The visit, taking place around Christmas time, appeared

The visit, taking place around Christmas time, appeared
to mean a lot to Mrs A, who has never spent Christmas with M.

The journey back was quicker as we took a different route.
M again had a major temper tantrum on the train and Mrs A
appeared anxious about intervening. The train was very
crowded and M was hitting me, kicking out and trying to bite.
Mrs A eventually restrained M.

I spoke to Mrs A about the need to be firm in her manage-
ment of M and to talk to her about the rehabilitation plans
and to make a calendar covering the plans so that M could
make sense of it.

Next Visit: Day Visit

Mother and M going home on their own on 15 December.

I have encouraged Mrs A to travel the quicker route; she is
reluctant to do so because of the need to change trains twice.
She appears to recognize the need to plan the journey more
carefully. She is keen to leave very early in the morning so as
to have the maximum time at home. I feel that the first visit
should take place over a couple of hours, rather than a whole
day. The time spent could be increased gradually.

Mother was obviously much happier once rehabilitation proper was
under way and she was much more in touch with her daughter. At
the review meeting in February, the following points were noted.

NOTES ON THE REVIEW OF MRS A: FEBRUARY

Nurse

The focus had been on the rehabilitation plans for Mrs A and
M to stay in their own home. This had entailed one accompanied visit, three day visits and four overnight stays. These
had gone well and Mrs A's relationships with others in the
community had improved as a result. However, she had found it
difficult to negotiate the progressive withdrawal of M's
contact from the foster mother rather than a complete break.
There had been some contact from her ex-husband, who had sent
her some of his drawings. Mrs A felt unfairly blamed for
things for which he was responsible, but she was able to
explain to M about the first child.

The relationship with her nurse had been difficult following the change. The nurse felt Mrs A tended to keep a distance
and be rather defensive. This was an outstanding difficulty.

Therapist

Therapy had continued twice weekly. This had gone well and Mrs A was more in touch with the issues about her ex-husband and the first child, though it remained hard for her to evaluate her early relationship with Mr A in light of subsequent events. Mrs A was able to express more of her anxieties about any contact with him, the rehabilitation plans and the difficulties of the relationship with the foster parents. At times, she was afraid of things going badly wrong and having to remain at the Cassel. When she felt overwhelmed by these anxieties, her tendency was to try and become controlling.

Child Therapy

Since the change in therapist, the latter had seen M and her mother together eight times over the last two months. The change in therapist had initially been difficult and M would express her feelings about this change most frequently by swearing. However, this had now improved, so that M played easily with her therapist at the beginning of the session and could express her feelings of loss regarding her previous therapist much more easily. However, there remained work to do on these matters.

A predominant theme was M's confusion about which home she should go to: she felt she had three. In the sessions, Mrs A demonstrated awareness of M's needs, related well to her, and the relationship between mother and child had become much warmer since the overnight stays at home and their spending much more time together. M became very upset at any mention of her father. Mrs A's planning of the withdrawal from the foster parents seemed to include a greater awareness of the feelings of loss this involved. She was also aware of her own pain and loss, particularly of the period in which M was in care, and similarly had some awareness of the effect on the foster mother of M returning to Mrs A.

At a planning meeting the previous day with social services, Mrs A's lack of trust was very apparent but plans needed to be worked out on a joint basis in a cooperative way. Also, the awareness of the feelings around loss and separation needed to include her leaving the Cassel and this should be properly worked through rather than being premature.

Nursery

M attends the nursery four times each week, is a lively child and behaves in a very age-appropriate way. She listens to stories and draws. She has had a tendency to be sulky when waiting for her turn and did have some tantrums with other children before Christmas but, in the last month, is more able to say sorry when she is aggressive and demonstrates guilt if she is told off for something. She is less anxious than she was about visits home.

In Mothers and Toddlers group, where Mrs A and M had been once a week, again this has been much more useful and has shown how mother and child can be much more spontaneous together. Mrs A can also set appropriate limits for M.

Dr Kennedy

He has seen major changes in his contact in firm meetings with Mrs A between last September and January. Previously, he observed a very distant relationship between mother and child, a lack of contact which had now become transformed. M he saw as lively, active, demanding and warm. Mrs A could set appropriate limits for her.

Mrs A

She felt the rehabilitation programme had completely transformed her relationship with M. She no longer felt there was a gap between them. She had been upset by the previous day's planning meeting and wanted a quicker rehabilitation plan to reduce the confusion for M. She admitted to difficulties in her relationship with the nurse and that she seemed to be able to talk to other staff instead. She wondered whether the nurse might represent a negative mother for her, but she did want to get on good terms with her, especially as the ending of her stay at the Cassel approached. She also felt she was able to express her upset about her first child in the hospital, but not carry over these feelings back to her new home and was more able to make a fresh start. She said that M now slept through the night at home and wanted to stay there, sometimes being angry towards the 'big house'. She felt her relationship with M was more open and that they could both express their frustration with each other.

Social Services

The new social worker expressed a firm commitment to the rehabilitation plans for Mrs A and was concerned to help as much as possible. This new worker had previously been the worker for the first child and it was recognized that this would cause Mrs A difficulty, but the new social worker had the advantage of knowing the full circumstances about the family. They would support as short a period of rehabilitation as possible, compatible with good care. They felt it would be easier to monitor home visits during the week as resources were not available at weekends.

The family care worker, who knew Mrs A, felt she had worked hard to make a home and now M treats it as her own home, toys being transferred from the foster mother's house, and she felt the mother–child relationship was very much improved.

Discussion

Questions were raised about Mrs A's negative feelings towards her nurse and although it was recognized that the changes of nurse and therapist had made for many difficulties, Mrs A's tendency to have negative feelings about some members of staff closely responsible for her was felt to be significant, particularly when combined with her tendency to swing from a defensive attitude, on the one hand, to a feeling that everything was perfectly all right, on the other. It was noted that her relationships with men had not yet particularly figured in therapy and possible future relationships with men in the community was an important matter which needed further therapy and monitoring when Mrs A returned home.

Rehabilitation Plan

Proposals had been put forward by the treatment team to reduce the contact and overnight stays with the foster mother and a plan for weekend stays. The team suggested a more flexible approach, recognizing that the first stage of rehabilitation was well under way and going well, but wishing to safeguard the remaining needs for therapy. The following points were made:

1. Treatment should continue until approximately May/June, part-way through the summer term, with discharge being

well in advance of the summer holiday so that community contact could be well established.

2. M's staying overnight with the foster mother should cease soon, but day-time contact should continue.

3. There should be work towards a pattern of perhaps two out of three weekends at home.

4. Regular monitoring visits were not required, but there should remain a commitment of perhaps one random visit to maintain the idea of contact.

5. There should be no question yet of any contact between M and her sibling, but some details, such as contact with Mrs A's own parents should be approached in a flexible and common-sense way.

The final rehabilitation plan was drawn up, though in the end there were a few minor changes to it.

REHABILITATION PLAN: SECOND STAGE: MRS A AND M

Weekend:

10 February	Mother and M at Cassel.
17 February	Mother and M first weekend at home. M seeing foster mother 2-6 p.m. Saturday.
24 February	Mother and M full weekend at home.
4 March	Mother and M at Cassel.
11 March	Mother and M at home for full weekend. M to see foster mother 2-6 p.m. Saturday.
18 March	Mother and M at home for full weekend.
25 March	Mother and M at Cassel for weekend.
31 March	Mother and M at home full weekend. M to see foster mother 5-6 p.m.

Review 6 April	**Proposed plan**
Weekend:	Following review, short visits with foster mother.
7 April	Full weekend at home.
Easter 13 April	Full weekend at home. ?4–5 days at home.
19 April	Short visit/meeting with foster mother, ? 1 hour.
21 April	Weekend at Cassel.
28 April	Full weekend at home.
6 May	Full weekend at home. ? Meet briefly with foster mother.
13 May	? Last Cassel weekend.

Details from the child therapy reports over this last period of treatment indicate what M was going through as discharge began to loom as a reality.

CHILD THERAPY REVIEW 1

I have been seeing M with her mother once-weekly for two months. There have been a number of missed sessions due to overnight visits to Mrs A's flat and again at Christmas time, so I have seen them for eight sessions only. When I first started to see them, they were both struggling to come to terms with a change of nurse and a change of therapist.

At the beginning of therapy, M seemed to use swearing as a way of expressing her anger at the loss of her former therapist. Her struggle to get to know a new therapist seemed to be expressed by a need to push me away verbally. She was able to talk about her previous therapist and acknowledge that she missed her. She is still at the stage of working through the loss, but now she greets me enthusiastically and relates to me well. She usually starts the session by coming to play with me for a few minutes; she then plays with her mother for the rest of the session. She no longer swears in her sessions.

The material that M has brought to her sessions recently

seems to express this little girl's struggle and confusion in coming to terms with the number of homes she visits and the number of times she gets ready to go there and return again to the hospital.

Recently, Mrs A seems to be very much more in touch with her own infantile feelings and acknowledges that there are times when she feels the need to be looked after. I feel that this is an indication that she can be more in touch with M's infantile parts. She responds well to M in the session and plays well with her. Since M has spent overnight visits in Mrs A's home, I have noticed a greater warmth between mother and daughter.

There have been a number of occasions when M became quite upset recently when we talked about her father. Mrs A was able to comfort M in a very loving and sensitive way. Mrs A is obviously thinking and planning ahead as regards M's eventual separation from the foster mother. She is aware of how damaging it might be to M if contact with the foster mother is stopped too suddenly. She also seems to be aware of both M's and foster mother's feelings in separating. Mrs A noticed recently how upset M had been at saying goodbye to foster mother after a recent weekend stay. She acknowledged that M seemed to be feeling the pangs of the beginning of the separation process.

The impatience that Mrs A is feeling about her rehabilitation plan and her consequent upset reaction when workers suggest that there is a need to take the process slowly, cannot help but communicate itself to M. It obviously affects M to see her mother upset. However, I think Mrs A is in touch with M's feelings and she tries her best to shield her from witnessing her distress.

It seems to me that the details of the preparation for rehabilitation of Mrs A and M need to be thought out carefully and taken slowly as a gradual process in which both mother and daughter will feel supported by the workers in order to gain the confidence and strength needed to face all the changes and struggles ahead. It is important that Mrs A consults with all the workers involved with her in this process so that she becomes aware that the rehabilitation is a joint effort. In this way, Mrs A will feel more contained and M will benefit as a result. It is important that the process is not cut off too suddenly so that enough space is created to enable mother and daughter to think and work through feelings of separation from the Cassel after so long a stay. I sympathize with Mrs A's need to try to speed things up. In a way, I see it as a healthy development, since she is enthusiastic in setting up a life for herself in the outside community. However, in her enthusiasm, she may not want to stop and think how best the process, if taken at a slightly slower pace, might help M and herself to adjust better to the challenge of adapting to life in the community outside. Perhaps she needs to be aware of how damaging it might be both to herself and to M if the treatment was cut off prematurely for the sake of a number of extra weeks which might facilitate them both being able to feel strongly supported in facing the outside world.

CHILD THERAPY REVIEW 2

Since the last Review on 9 February, I have seen M with her mother once weekly. I was absent for three weeks, so I have seen them five times only.

M has brought to the sessions some of her more difficult emotions concerned with all the changes that are taking place in her life at the moment. She is angry and puzzled at having slowly to relinquish her bond with her foster mother, whom she has known since birth. She is also confused and feeling that there is an injustice about it all.

Some of M's and her mother's most agonizing feelings came to a head when there was a meeting arranged on 21 March in order to give some support to the foster mother. The nurse and myself met with the foster mother whilst Mrs A and M met with Mrs A's social worker. At the end of our meeting with the foster mother, we all met together.

It became obvious at the end of this meeting, when I had a short session with M and her mother, how much pain, heartbreak and confusion M is feeling at this time as she is gradually 'weaned off' her foster mother and is seeing more of her mother. It was also clear how painful it was for Mrs A to observe the very close bond between her daughter and the foster mother. She felt 'torn apart' by this, yet she was able to face and acknowledge in words what she actually felt and, in spite of her own very deep pain, was able to comfort M in a warm, sympathetic way at the point when M had just said goodbye to her foster mother and was finding it hard to understand why she had had to go away again.

Our work together since that date has been to work through the painful feelings experienced by both mother and daughter. In spite of the difficult feelings that did emerge from this meeting, it was productive in the sense that these are the real feelings central to their lives at the moment and they were brought out and worked with. We are planning to have one more meeting with the foster mother, who felt that since she had known M since birth, she might have been more included in M's treatment from the beginning of the admission to the Cassel. She had felt hurt and unsupported at being left out.

I think a further meeting would be helpful in order to contain some of the more angry attacking feelings coming from Mrs A and the foster mother, which seem to be a way of not feeling the pain which inevitably is there in negotiating the resolving of these changing relationships for M.

There is a feeling communicated by M that things are 'not fair'. It seems, at the moment, that all her own internal objects are confused and she is going through a very painful time of separating them out in her mind as she separates from her first attachment figure.

In spite of all that M has to negotiate emotionally, I feel that she is a very resilient little girl who continues to be outgoing. However, I do feel that her outgoing and charming personality can mask the deep pain that she is feeling inside and it is important that all the staff are aware of what a difficult time it is for M at the moment.

In the last phase of treatment, it became more possible to think about Mrs A's choice of men and her fear of future relationships and trusting somebody again in case they would turn out to be like Mr A. Mrs A was more able to acknowledge the way that she compartmentalizes her life and keeps things manageable by being very controlling and trying to keep everybody very separate. She was also able to see how, throughout her life, she has wished to be 'ahead of herself', to live up to her own very high expectations of herself and her great fear of failure which leads her to attempt to maintain a very perfect front for the outside world. Mrs A was able to use the experience of ending at the hospital in a very constructive way, to think about building a new relationship with her family on a more adult level and also to be in touch with the loss of support and relationships here which have been very important to her.

In the last two to three months prior to discharge, Mrs A spent every weekend at home with M and on alternate weeks these lasted for three nights, rather than two. She was able to arrange for M to start pre-school for the second half of the summer term and was able to introduce M to her new school. M gradually saw less of her foster mother and Mrs A was able to manage these visits in a way that was helpful for M.

M's name was removed from the At Risk register, having been listed under the category of physical abuse. However, M remained on the care order and work was done in the last few weeks in planning supervision by social services after discharge. Mrs A's parents came to an extended family meeting just prior to discharge and were able to listen to Mrs A's concerns for the future: her worries that she feels excluded from the family and not able to fulfil her parent's expectations of her. Mrs A was able to manage her goodbyes both from the community and the staff in a way that felt helpful and constructive.

Recommendations for follow-up were made at the last review before discharge in April:

1. M should be assessed for therapy by local child and family services, either individually or with Mrs A.

2. Mrs A should consider further therapy herself; although at present she does not feel that she would like to continue with therapy, she may find it helpful in the future.

3. The Family Unit would offer a follow-up appointment for Mrs A and M in three months' time to consider their progress and needs for the future. This meeting could include their social worker for part of the time, if she would like to attend.

4. M met with her sister prior to discharge. This was the first time they had seen each other in some time and the first time ever that Mrs A had seen the two of her children together. It is planned that these meetings would continue and M will, therefore, need particular help in dealing with issues around her having a sister who does not live with her, and so on.

5. Access between M and Mr A may become an issue in the future although, for the time being, access is limited to postal contact only. This may be an area that Mrs A will need help to think about in the future.

Several months later, Mrs A and M had the opportunity of seeing the original child psychotherapist who had returned from maternity leave. The therapist wrote that:

M came in to see me with her mother. She is a lot taller now and she was wearing a very pretty little jumper and a badge saying 'Four Years'. She told me that she is now four, her birthday had been on Tuesday. She was pleased to see me again and began exploring all the toys in the room, remembering which she had played with. Mother was a bit uncomfortable at first, finding it difficult to come back to the hospital after all this time. However, she was able to tell me about the good things that were happening in the community: M now goes to playschool three times a week and mother had started a maths class. She hopes to begin midwifery training, which she has always wanted to do, in a couple of years' time. She says she loves her house and feels very settled there, and has good neighbours with little children around at weekends like M. Her relationship with social services has also improved and they have been able to say how pleased they are with the progress M had made. They are talking about revoking the care order. She says that she and M do have ups and downs, but she really enjoys being a mum at home with her. The evenings are much easier now and M goes to bed between 7.30 and 8.00 p.m. Certainly M seems a delightful little girl; calm and interested in everything in the room and able to tell me about her friend at school and how she wanted to go to 'big school' soon.

One could see from this report that mother and M had made enormous progress since they had left the hospital and that M's development seemed excellent. Mother was gradually beginning to feel that the authorities do trust her and that she is a good mother; she was beginning to be able to relax and recognize that she had been able to use the help that she was offered at the Cassel Hospital, although she was very glad it was over. The progress has been maintained since that time.

6 DESTRUCTIVE BEHAVIOUR IN THE FAMILY

In many of the families treated at the Cassel, destructive behaviour has come to dominate the family's life. This chapter will examine some general issues around destructiveness in families through a psychoanalytic perspective, as well as some more specific issues concerning physical abuse in families.

THE FAMILY IN LITERATURE

One could say that the result of destructive behaviour in the family is one of the dominant themes of many of the key works of Western literature. Attention paid to some of this literature may open up themes which can help us to understand some of the predicaments of modern families. Such literature often involves distorted relationships between one generation and another, or a refusal to accept the reality of one family member, or else the fear of one family member's power over the others. Destructive forces played out within the family can also be used to represent a society torn apart or breaking up. Alternatively, as for example in Dostoevsky's *The Brothers Karamazov*, a family tragedy can become the focus for tackling wider issues of the nature of existence and belief. His compatriot Tolstoy, concerned with wider issues but also with the relationship between families and their society, begins his great novel *Anna Karenina* by stating that: 'All happy families are like one another; each unhappy family is unhappy in its own way.' He charts how Anna Karenina's bid for freedom outside the family leads in the end to her destruction.

A number of Greek tragedies touch on the intimate relationship between powerful families and their society. Thus, in the *Oresteia* of Aeschylus, the haughty Agamemnon sacrifices the life of his daughter in order to placate the gods and obtain fair weather for the Greek fleet's voyage to Troy. The result of this attack on his daughter is that after he returns home, he is killed by his wife who, in turn, is later killed by their son, Orestes. The latter is then driven mad by the consequences of his act, and is pursued by the avenging furies. However, at the end of the *Oresteia*, there is a resolution of the conflict when Orestes is purified of the murder and the furies are transformed into guardian spirits of Athens. One could say that there has been a sublimation of the dark, destructive forces. The curse of Orestes' family is also laid to rest; this curse arose as a consequence of a vile act in which Atreus, father of Agamemnon, killed the children of his brother Thyestes and served them to him at a dinner. He did so because Thyestes had seduced Atreus' wife. When Thyestes discovered what he had eaten, he cursed his brother's family. Later, it was Aegisthus, son of Thyestes, who helped to kill Agamemnon. In *Oedipus Turannos*, Oedipus is maimed and left to die because he poses a threat to his father; but, as we all know, neither could escape his fate. The consequences of such an attack on a baby led to the father's murder and to incest with the mother.

In a sense, these and other Greek tragedies are about a particular model of reason which involves people relating harmoniously to one another in a community. Once the harmony is disturbed through, for example, attacks on family structure or on society's rules or kinship structures, then families and those around them are exposed to powerful destructive forces. The ancient Greek notion of rationality is complex and not to be understood as some simple model in which reason rules over passion. Rather, Plato and Aristotle, for example, conceived of the reasoning person as part of a wider community with whom he or she is subtly connected. In this model, there are divisions within the psyche and interaction between these parts; there is a dynamic relationship between reason and unreason, and between the individual and his community or polis. The Greek individual is close to the public world and less cut off than ourselves from others. Thus, when there is a crisis within the family, when harmony between family members is disturbed, when destructive forces are unleashed as in many tragedies, there are major repercussions on the community. One may well ask whether we are currently witnessing a similar impact on our own community with the increasing attention being turned on those families who have abused their children.

Another theme from ancient Greek comedy and the Roman plays of Plautus and Terence, through to Shakespeare and Molière, is that of the central role of the father in families. There was a notion that the father's role was clear. He was important, a VIP. As Shakespeare put it, in *A Midsummer Night's Dream*:

> To you your father should be as a god;
> One that compos'd your beauties, yea, and one
> To whom you are but as a form in wax
> By him imprinted, and within his power
> To leave the figure, or disfigure it ...
> ... your eyes must with his judgement look. (Act 1, sc. 2)

Of course, Shakespeare showed how such a narrow-minded attitude only leads to despair and confusion, which results in the mix-up of lovers in the Athenian woods, and, happily, a final resolution. The plays of Molière are also full of the absurdities of fathers who attempt to dictate to their children how they should behave and whom they should marry. Perfect obedience, the plays seem to show, only leads to disaster. Job, in the Bible, was a good if extreme example of a man who obeyed God perfectly, denying his own capacity to destroy. Suppression of his own destructiveness led to the loss of his family and possessions. Only when he had faced the reality of the devil's temptations could his fortunes be restored.

Shakespeare also revealed the darker side of the father in, for example, *King Lear*. The tragedy can be understood at many levels, but one relevant theme is that of distorted family relationships. Of his three daughters, Cordelia is the absolute favourite. However, Lear loves her in a monstrously possessive fashion. When it comes to the dividing of his kingdom, he wishes her to put her love for him above all other loves which, of course, she cannot do if she is to become a woman. The sisters, Goneril and Regan, used to being in Cordelia's shadow, are now used to hypocrisy and can pretend their love is exclusive, and Lear does not mind one way or the other. In fact these sisters, deprived of their father's love and witnesses of his possessive attachment to Cordelia, become hypocritical monsters and ultimately die over their wish to possess the illegitimate Edmund. Edmund himself is deprived of his father's presence. When the play opens, his father, the Duke of Gloucester, who will later be blinded, tells how Edmund has to remain distant from his father: 'He hath been out nine years, and away he shall again' (Act 1, sc. 1).

Edmund seeks vengeance by displacing the true-born Edgar. The play, then, seems to revolve around the question of the father's role, and reveals the disastrous and destructive consequences when this role is distorted; when, for example, the father is possessive or shows undue favouritism, is absent or where there is no mother to soften the father's harsh authority.

WHAT IS DESTRUCTIVE BEHAVIOUR?

Psychoanalytic and other thinkers seem to have very different views about the nature of aggressiveness and destructiveness. Some thinkers consider man as naturally destructive; others that man only learns to be destructive, but is naturally peaceful. Some analysts, following Freud and Klein, believe in an inborn death instinct; others that there is no evidence of any such instinct, and that the infant's behaviour reveals, on the contrary, dominant impulses turned positively towards the world, long before there are signs of destructiveness. Freud, in 'Civilization and its Discontents', considered that civilized society is perpetually threatened with disintegration because of the primary mutual hostility between human beings (1930, p. 112). Man must learn how to renounce his innate destructive drives if he is to become civilized. But there is a constant conflict between the desire to be destructive and the needs of the community, which causes considerable frustration, and is a basic cause of man's susceptibility to neurosis.

Such a view is not dissimilar to that of the British philosopher, Hobbes, who believed that man was by nature essentially egoistic, and that each individual, if left to his own devices, seeks his own conservation. This leads to competition with, and envy of, others. This view contrasts with, for example, that of Rousseau who believed that man was born free and was naturally good, and that society put him in chains. These differing views of man's nature are concerned with the question of virtue and vice. Some thinkers, like Hobbes, seem to consider man as naturally full of vices; others, such as Joseph Butler, consider that virtue corresponds to our nature, while vice violates it. In the latter viewpoint, vice, evil and destructiveness go against our nature in some way, rather as in Greek tragedy the main characters often seem to go against the order of the world.

There is also a considerable literature concerned with the nature of aggression, which discusses, among other things, the degree to which aggression is biologically useful. Erich Fromm, in his book *The Anatomy of Human Destructiveness*, (1974) makes the useful distinction between benign and malignant aggression. The former is biologically adaptive and life-serving, while the latter is nonadaptive. Benign aggression is not necessarily destructive, while malignant aggression is characterized by the wish to destroy for the sake of destruction. 'Only man,' Fromm wrote, 'seems to take pleasure in destroying life without any reason or purpose other than that of destroying. To put it more generally, only man appears to be destructive beyond the aim of defence or of attaining what he needs' (pp. 252–3).

Although it is difficult to be precise about terms in this particular field of enquiry, it might be useful, if only for convenience, to classify destructive phenomena seen in the psychoanalytic field into (i) destructive impulses and fantasies; (ii) destructive acts; and (iii) mixtures of destructive impulses and acts.

Destructive Impulses and Fantasies

In this category, one could put various attacks directed on the patient's self, with varying degrees of disintegration and fragmentation of personality structure, but without actual attacks on the patient's body or on others. As the work of Bion, Winnicott and others has shown, accompanying destructive fantasies and impulses there may be different degrees of dissociation, splitting and lack of integration of the psyche. Excessive destructiveness may be accompanied by extensive and pathological projection. There may be varying mixtures of self and/or object destructiveness.

Melanie Klein considered that destructive impulses were present from birth, and were partly projected outward, by means of a deflection of the innate death instinct, and attached themselves to the mother's breast. For her, the threat of annihilation by the death instinct within was the primordial anxiety with which the infant has to deal. The infant's ego, which is in the service of the life instinct, then attempts to deflect the threat outwards. The various processes of splitting and fragmenting of the ego and its objects represent attempts to disperse the destructive impulses. She conceived that, in the normal child, there is a gradual process of integration, in which the infant builds up an image of a good whole object. However, if there is an excess of destructive impulses there may be a major interference with the building up of the good object, with a consequent predisposition to severe mental disturbance (Klein, 1957).

Winnicott, in contrast, emphasized the need for the infant to be taken by the mother through a period of destructiveness. The mother is, in phantasy, constantly being destroyed or damaged.

The child gradually comes to integrate the loved and the damaged mother. The mother's capacity to survive the attacks is important; thus Winnicott placed emphasis on the positive value of destructiveness. The fact that the mother can survive the attacks places her outside the child's omnipotent control and offers a basis for shared reality (Winnicott, 1963, 1969). Hate could also be seen in some people as a way of keeping themselves from falling apart.

Destructive Acts

Destructive acts are no doubt often accompanied by destructive fantasies, but not all such fantasies are directly enacted in reality. There would seem to be particular kinds of destructive acts which need to be thought about in a special way. Such acts include child physical and sexual abuse, murder, substance abuse and severe criminality. These acts not infrequently take place directly within the context of the family, and thus are particularly relevant to the theme of this book.

Mixtures of Destructive Impulses and Acts

In this category, one could place suicidal behaviour, acts of self-mutilation and sado-masochism. These phenomena appear to involve destructive fantasies, but usually there has to be an accompanying act in order for the fantasy to be expressed; imagination alone is not usually sufficient. There are also some people who seem to have destructive personalities. They are compelled to ruin their careers and/or their relationships. Destructiveness may here be a defence against loving. They are probably to be found within the diagnostic categories of borderline or narcissistic personalities.

DESTRUCTIVE ACTS IN THE FAMILY:
Further Thoughts on Child Physical Abuse

First of all, one could say that destructive acts in the family are more likely when the family's everyday structures have broken down. Rather than seeing destructive acts as leading to the breakdown of family structures, one could see the breakdown of these structures as leading to destructive behaviour.

One could further suggest that the destructive act of physical abuse has a purpose, a meaning. The abused child, at a particular moment of vulnerability – for example, when showing acute signs of distress or helplessness or signs of temper and separateness from the parent's control – is suddenly experienced by the parent as an enormous threat. The psychic pain shown by the helpless or out of control child cannot be tolerated by the abusing parent. The child is seen as all bad or destructive, and as taking away all the parent's goodness. The parent cannot experience the pain of the helpless child as it poses too much of a threat to the parent's self. There would also often seem to be a vengeful aspect to the physical attack. The damage done to the child is a revenge for the psychic and/or physical damage done to the parents when they were children. The particular cruelty or malignancy sometimes shown by the abusing parent to the victim, however much the violent act may take place in a sudden fit of temper, seems to be as a result of the unconscious need to have revenge for the neglected child in themselves. A yearning for care is stirred up in the parents when their own children show signs of helplessness as well as signs that they are separate from their parents, and such yearnings become an immediate threat to the parents' sense of self.

Why are these parents so threatened by dependency? As previously mentioned, they themselves have often experienced a childhood in which they were either beaten or unloved, or else never had a parent or parent figure who kept them in mind in a centrally focused way. They have also frequently had a stormy and difficult adolescence, which has predisposed them to difficulties in coping with violence and depression. One might expect these factors to have produced a particular deformation in their super-ego structure. Freud, in 'Civilization and its Discontents', discussed the origin of the sense of guilt and of the super-ego. He pointed out that before the formation of the latter, the child begins to distinguish good from bad by means of external influences, as a result of the parents' restrictions, punishment, and so on. But, he asked, what is the motive for yielding to the parents' influence and not wishing to have all their drives satisfied? Freud suggested that:

Such a motive is easily discovered in his helplessness and his dependence on other people, and it can best be designated as fear of loss of love. If he loses the love of another person upon whom he is dependent, he also ceases to be protected from a variety of dangers. Above all, he is exposed to the danger that his stronger person will show his superiority in the form of punishment. At the beginning, therefore, what is bad is whatever causes one to be threatened with loss of love. For fear of that loss, one must avoid it. (1930, p. 124)

A change then arises when the authority is internalized through the establishment of the structured super-ego. 'The phenomena of conscience then reach a higher stage. Actually,' Freud wrote,

it is not until now that we should speak of conscience or a sense of guilt. At this point, too, the fear of being found out comes to an end; the distinction, moreover, between doing something bad and wishing to do it disappears entirely, since nothing can be hidden from the super-ego. (1930, p. 125)

Thus, there are two origins for the sense of guilt – the early fear of an authority, and the later fear of the super-ego. First there was renunciation of drives owing to fear of aggression and loss of love by the external authority; and then came the later erection of an internal authority, the super-ego and renunciation of drives through fear of it. The process involved in internalization seems to be that the child, by means of identification, takes the external authority into him- or herself.

The authority now turns into his super-ego and enters into possession of all the aggressiveness which the child would have liked to exercise against it ... the original severity of the super-ego does not ... represent the original severity which one has experienced from ... [the object], or which one attributes to it; it represents one's own aggressiveness to it. (1930, p. 129–30)

How are we then to understand the psychical situation in the child abuser? First of all, by and large, they have experienced severe upbringings, or else have largely been unloved. Although Freud, like Klein, emphasized that the harshness of the super-ego is not necessarily related to the reality of a harsh parent, he did suggest that a harsh upbringing exerts a strong influence on the formation of the child's super-ego. Not only will the child identify with a harsh parent, but their own innate aggressiveness will not be appropriately modified by adequate caring and love. The normal suppression of considerable amounts of aggressiveness will not take place, and the whole process of internalization and super-ego formation will be distorted, as they have had real experiences of loss of love.

Hence, as adults with their own children, they cannot bear the child's expression of helplessness and need for them, so that there are times when the social work agency has to take over the role as authority for the child. The child's expression of pain may be perceived by the parent as a sign that they are taking away all the good from the parent; a feeling that unfortunately may have to be confirmed when they are under threat of losing a child. One could add here in structural terms that, with an imperfectly formed super-ego, there is a consequent limitation on the ego's structure, a blindness to need and a lack of responsiveness to the child.

One can also see, at times, how hate for the child can have a perversely binding function for the adults. Aggression towards the child may help to bind together the parents in love. While the child receives the aggressiveness, the parents appear to love one another. Some of the parents we treat really have to learn to fall in love with their children, as if they were newborn.

Treatment of these families involves not only recognition of some of the dynamics outlined above, but also requires detailed attention to any legal structures imposed on the family. Once the authorities act as parents to a child, they will to some extent arouse feelings and yearnings that the parents did not experience as children. Yet the parents usually fight these yearnings and deny any sense of dependency on the authorities, complaining instead of being persecuted. The authorities, they say, are the ones who are abusing and destructive. It is usually humiliating and persecuting for the parents openly to acknowledge any dependency needs. But if rehabilitation is to succeed, and if the parents are to take back responsibility for the children, as we aim to do in the Family Unit, the facing of these issues is fundamental.

Clinical Example

The following brief example may illustrate some of these points on child abuse.

The 'A' Family were admitted to the Family Unit some years ago as their three-year-old boy had been physically abused by his mother, was a Ward of Court and living in a foster home. An older daughter was living with the parents. The mother herself had had a violent upbringing. In addition, she had to undress in front of her father, while he examined her, into her twenties. It was noticeable that, on admission, she tended to walk around the Unit in quite blatant flimsy clothing, until this was actively pointed out.

Her husband, though physically strong, was a somewhat passive man, still dependent on his own mother, and unable to intervene to stop his wife from damaging his son. He stood by as if helpless while his wife beat the boy.

As a result of our assessment, we thought we could offer treatment as there had been some limited change, but only on certain conditions. We needed a tight legal framework, which at that time, before the Children Act, included Wardship for the daughter, whom we discovered to be just as much at risk, and that she be placed with the foster home until we could work towards rehabilitation for the whole family. Our recommendations were challenged by the parents, with the active involvement of the father's mother. Their lawyers attempted to dispute some of the less important recommendations. However, we had become used to such situations, which in fact have tended to lessen over the years, as links with the legal profession have increasingly grown. These families, anyway, not infrequently seem to have to test staff out in this way. As they allowed themselves to be forced into a confrontation, the family became increasingly dangerous in the hospital. This danger was resolved when the court hearing took place and our conditions were accepted by the lawyers and the Judge, and eventually the parents, as a result of considerable work in the corridors of the court with myself and both sets of lawyers.

Although the framework was agreed, treatment was still difficult. The mother revealed considerable difficulties in most aspects of daily life, and was unable to play with the children. She demanded that the children behave, and saw any helplessness they might display as evidence of how they robbed her of goodness. There were constant worrying episodes, with situations of near physical violence. At one of our regular review meetings, which included their social worker, it was discovered that the various workers had spent so much time dealing with these crises that there had hardly been any time to do the usual psychotherapeutic and nursing work in the ordinary work of the day. As a result, and in spite of the social services' initial opposition, more efforts were directed at getting on with ordinary treatment. What made us think that it was worthwhile carrying on was that the father in particular made some major steps. He was able to become more separate from his own mother, and was more able to intervene when his wife lost control. The couple's sexual life came more into the open and the family eventually made substantial progress. They were all returned to their home for weekends, and were successfully rehabilitated.

This family, like so many others in similar situations where there is the risk of real destructive behaviour, aroused considerable anxiety in workers. Successful rehabilitation of such families who, at first sight, seem beyond treatment, depends on the capacity of the workers around a family to understand, monitor and deal effectively with this anxiety. It is inevitable that workers will feel anxious about these cases; it can be even more worrying when they do not feel anxious, for this may indicate some denial of the family's difficulties or dangers.

In order to deal with their anxieties, as already suggested, there need to be clear lines of professional responsibility, effective communication between workers, and an atmosphere in which mutual trust can be promoted. In this kind of work, it is also important for the workers to be committed to the families even if, in the end, they recommend that the children be separated from their parents. That is, there needs to be a large measure of advocacy of parents' and children's rights. Without this sense of commitment, which comes from having effective structures for metabolizing staff anxieties, the destructiveness that inevitably accompanies these families can merely be repeated in the workers. Work with these families, in simple terms, involves converting destructive behaviour into workable communication difficulties, changing behaviour into words and destructive acts into relationship difficulties which can then be treated. Such work should also take place with the assumption that workers are trying to develop a trusting relationship with them. These are often families where trust has broken down and where they may never have experienced a trusting relationship. One could argue that there is all the more reason to offer them a chance to work through their previous disappointments, but this means facing considerable amounts of destructiveness.

7 FEMALE ABUSERS

The fact that there are female abusers is still shocking, as workers continue to find that mothers can and do seriously harm
their children. After all, it goes against the powerful image of
mother as protector and provider of warmth and security. Harm
in this context refers to major damage, for example, when there
has been such a violent attack on a child that it has been killed
or paralysed, or severely bruised; when a child has been repeatedly sexually molested by the mother or her partner, or when
there has been severe poisoning of a child.

Are these women just victims of their own past, a past where
more often than not they were severely abused as children? Do
they just get caught up with some violent man whom they cannot
abandon? Or are some of them just evil? Can we possibly understand what happens when a woman batters her child, ignores its
screams induced by a partner's brutal attack, or when she has sex
with her son or daughter, or allows someone else to molest them?

Attitudes towards these problems seem to have changed quite
remarkably in recent years. Thanks to, for example, the pioneering
work of Estela Welldon (1988), the idealization of women and
motherhood has shifted. To suggest, only about five years ago at,
say, a conference, that women can be active abusers would have
been to risk being subjected to attack for being chauvinistic and
anti-women. It was just not politically correct at that time to
describe what the Cassel was seeing.

There is, no doubt, much we do not understand; but what
follows is a picture of some of these women, admittedly on the
more extreme end of the spectrum. In this chapter there will be an
account of a woman who was complicit in severe physical violence,
and a family with sexual abuse as the main problem. Though there
is probably a wide variety of such situations, it is possible to see
certain common patterns begin to emerge; though, again, one must
emphasize our continuing ignorance.

There would seem to be at least three major, and probably
overlapping, categories of female abusers: the 'active abuser', who

is the main instigator and perpetrator; the 'complicit abuser', or 'inciter', who takes part in the attack but does not instigate it directly, and instead incites the partner to abuse; and the 'denier', who does not want to believe that her partner has abused their child or children. The denier, as with the others, may also be intimidated by the partner. But with the really difficult cases, intimidation is often fairly mutual, if one can put it like that. One should also say here that the male perpetrator does not have to be an obviously violent thug. He is just as likely to be a rather passive and apparently unassuming person, heavily dependent on his partner – what one might call the 'violent wimp'. The woman, frequently a denier, often has to prop him up, but then his seething resentment about his partner's power over him may suddenly erupt into violence. The child is attacked, because it is the most sadistic way of getting at the woman, but also because he is so dependent on her. These kinds of men may be difficult to treat. However, experience at the hospital is often that the male perpetrator of physical abuse who has been incited by his partner may be more able to use therapy. In terms of numbers in these different categories, the majority of women we have seen where there has been child abuse are either inciters or deniers. Though we have assessed a few active sexually abusing women, for one reason or another they have not been involved in treatment, mainly because their and their family's pathology have been so extreme that we have recommended removal of their children. Other workers, particularly at the Portman Clinic, may have a wider experience than I of the active sexual abuser. But we have seen quite a number of women who have incited or denied sexual abuse, and a considerable number who have been active physical abusers. There have also been a number of women who have displayed inappropriate sexualized contact with their children, but have not apparently actually sexually abused the children themselves directly, though they may have turned a blind eye to their partner's more extreme behaviour. But, in the end, it is likely that these distinctions do not have that much explanatory value; furthermore, they might also give a false impression that being an active abuser is somehow much worse than, say, giving your child to someone else to abuse. There is not much to choose in terms of horror between different ways of torturing a child.

To return to trying to understand what goes wrong in these families, one of the main themes one can find in a number of abusing women who themselves have been severely sexually abused as children, usually repeatedly, is a fundamental and 'impossible' conflict about being simultaneously a mother and a sexual woman. They seem to be put into an impossible situation, one which appears before treatment to have no solution except through some environmental action, often with the participation of a partner. Whenever they are put into the position of being a mother, having to look after a dependent child, at some point, particularly when there is the possibility of feeling vulnerable, they blank off their maternal feelings. To be a mother for these women means having to identify with their own neglectful mother, the one who allowed abuse to happen.

Since this is an almost impossible subjective position to occupy, they tend to blank out dependent feelings in themselves and their children. But, of course, this leaves them vulnerable to allowing abuse and to ignoring it, blanking out the reality of their children's suffering. Their model of parenting may have been one in which their own father, or substitute father, has turned to them instead of their mother for sexual satisfaction, as the mother has blocked out her own sexuality. They thus learn in turn to block off their sexuality, but again this will put their own child in a dangerous position of being potentially available to a man for sexual satisfaction and relief. A vicious circle of abuse is set up. It can feel maddening to be in the circle and to feel there is no way out of it. Also, these women may be very resistant to facing a move into a more benign sort of circle; there may be an intense and psychotic fear about disintegration, should they abandon old ways of relating.

The main aim of treatment is to try and break into this closed system, both by allowing the woman to face and understand her destructiveness and, at the same time, by helping her to face dependency issues more effectively.

Facing dependency sounds simple enough but, of course, it is fundamentally difficult for these women. One often does not see in them and their relationship with their children, the ordinary sort of dependent relations. Their own internal structures are so disorganized that they find it difficult to provide continuous care. Their children are not seen as providers of pleasure, except in distorted ways. Role reversal, with the child mothering the mother, is familiar; but the child may also be perceived in quite idiosyncratic ways as an adult, as a persecutor, as totally merged with themselves, or as a reminder of a hated partner. In their own histories, there has frequently been a series of major traumas, quite often with a home atmosphere of violence or extreme emotional turmoil. Under these circumstances, ordinary object relations with firm identifications are not build up. Instead, they are left with a precarious psychic structure. Possibly, violence and confusion have to be re-created in later life in order to feel alive. Feeling alive through various forms of violence – and for a woman her child may be the victim more often than another adult – may be a way of trying to overcome the blanking out of emotions mentioned before. The active sexually abusing woman in particular may have great difficulty in integrating in herself the sexual body with the pre-adolescent body. Her own body may feel damaged and unintegrated, even dead. The abuse of the child may be in part an act of revenge for her own past abuse, but also a crazy way of trying to make herself feel alive through sexual gratification. Doing this with another adult may not give the deep and primitive feeling of re-creating a childhood scenario. Also, one can unfortunately see how hatred for the child can have a sort of perversely organizing function for the adult. One can also see this in couples where aggression towards the child may help to bind the parents together.

SEVERE PHYSICAL ABUSE

Mrs X was originally admitted with her husband following the severe physical abuse of their oldest child. The latter received serious and disabling injuries from the father and was subsequently removed permanently from the parents. The younger child, a son aged two, was admitted with his parents for assessment. Initially, in the hospital, both parents kept very much to themselves. Mother seemed to relate reasonably well to her son, though she lacked spontaneity. Father expressed regrets about what had happened, but had little insight into his situation. He was rather impervious to attempts to help him understand himself and found it difficult to relate to other patients. Staff, particularly female nurses, found him intimidating. Behind the little boy facade, he was felt to be intrusive and unsavoury in some kind of way.

By the end of the assessment, we felt that the couple were unable to be worked with as together they showed little capacity to engage in treatment. The violence was tangible but constantly denied by the father, who maintained that everything had now changed and that he would never do anything like that again. The mother supported the father at first and could not speak out as a separate person. Yet, faced with the stark choice between her husband and her son, the mother, like that in the detailed clinical case in Chapter 5, chose the latter, a choice which is by no means obvious in a number of our families. We reassessed her and her son and eventually embarked on a slow process of rehabilitation.

The couple had become almost merged with one another, so that separation could only be achieved by some kind of violent process. Indeed, it was only after the trauma of a stark choice that the mother was able to separate from him. Even then it was a very rocky treatment for some time. She tended to deny aggressive feelings. She had done this before with her husband: on the one hand, knowing deep down that he was viciously maltreating their first child; yet, on the other hand, unable to face what she was doing by ignoring his violence. Also, and this is quite common in these situations, she had blanked off the memory of incidents where clearly the child was being abused. It was only much later, in therapy, that she began to piece together the memories of that time.

With her son, she was quite engaging, but always kept him at a distance. It was only when rehabilitation continued into her mother's new home that she felt finally able to have close physical and emotional contact with her son, who then became a lot happier. She was also then more able to talk about her own fear of hitting him severely.

Mother had never felt accepted by her own mother. Her father had always gone along with his wife's attitude, though clearly being troubled by it. Mrs X lost respect for him. She revealed major authority difficulties in the hospital, which she particularly and naturally focused on myself. It was as if she were constantly testing me to see if I was a 'weak father' who could not keep the staff in order. This dynamic also allowed her to get more in touch with her aggressive feelings, which she had tended to deny and project into others, including her abusing partner. She also experienced me as being dominated by the rather difficult social services department. These kinds of feelings were very useful for her treatment, and she did well and made some significant changes. She was no longer so secretly anti-authority and mistrustful of relationships. She was much more able to talk and to keep her child in mind. She began to feel that she could perceive when she might put herself and her son into a dangerous situation, rather than unconsciously seek it and then deny it.

SEXUAL ABUSE

Mrs X was, at first, too distant from her child; while Ms Y, who had been sexually abused repeatedly as a child and became a prostitute in adolescence, was much too enmeshed with her six-year-old son – so much so that she allowed him to be sexually abused by at least two male partners. Her history is only too familiar, with neglect, abuse and moving between children's homes. One could say that there is a danger for professionals that they hear these kinds of stories so often that they begin to cut off and ignore the person's individuality, as the patients do to themselves. Ms Y's prostitution allowed her not only to earn money and to revenge herself on men, but also to re-create a repeated abusing scenario in which she lost her own individuality and allowed her body to be attacked. At least one episode of anal abuse happened to her son while she was engaged in prostitution. She alleged that she had not realized that the client had attacked her son.

Despite the awful history, she had managed to seek help, and there was something resilient about her. She had an engaging honesty that did not seem to be aimed just at being seductive. Treatment was slow and stormy. Not surprisingly, she increasingly revealed her delinquent side in the hospital, becoming the frequent instigator of anti-therapeutic actions, allying herself with anyone who wanted to cause trouble. Yet she was also keen on letting her son be treated. He was a very disturbed boy, with major emotional and learning difficulties, who continued to have intensive therapy after discharge from the hospital. Typically, he was unable to concentrate for long, appeared over-excitable, was often disruptive and testing of boundaries, and he and his mother had an over-close and sexualized relationship. For example, he would try to touch her breasts repeatedly and she would do little to discourage him. Much of the therapeutic work was focused on trying to establish a less sexualized relationship between them. This was initially quite difficult as she did not perceive what was wrong in their contact.

Accompanying the sexualized contact, Ms Y revealed that she was very confused about child and adult elements in herself. Not surprisingly, she found dealing with dependency issues very difficult. There seemed to be an advantage in focusing much more on her mothering than on the rest of her personality. It would have been too great a task to think that she could have been transformed in the eighteen months or so that she was in the hospital. But by focusing on the key area of mothering, on trying to allow mother and son to be more separate and by constantly bringing her back to what she was avoiding in her mothering, we were able to facilitate some quite specific but definite positive changes in her. In people with such diffuse identifications, focal work can be surprisingly effective.

There is also the constant problem of sexualization of the transference. Emotional contact can often be confused with sexual contact. Ms Y, in fact, had a male individual therapist. This meant that these issues were brought directly into treatment. He was, at first, used by her and perceived in some ways as just another client, and was constantly denigrated. It took a long time to shift her basic lack of trust in him. The other areas that we were able to touch on were her delinquency and some of her destructive attitudes to her own body. The latter had resulted in allowing her son's body to be intruded upon.

The kind of issues we found with Ms Y seem to be common to several other families in which there has been severe sexual abuse. In these cases, one has to deal with issues of intense abandonment, mistrust, intrusion, and testing of boundaries and parental failure, all of which are repeated over and over in the treatment. Treatment of the abused and abusing woman may involve having to deal with 'abuse equivalents'. There is a repetition in the transference of the kind of parental care system around the child which led to the abuse. They themselves, as children, as in Ms Y's case, were subjected to significant impingement and breaks in the provision of continuous care. These gaps in the holding structure may be small enough to be glossed over, or kept just about intact by some kind of temporary repair. Or they may be so great as to cause major psychic damage. In treatment, the therapist may be seen as part of a constantly failing environment. There may also be, as was the case with Ms Y, a wish to keep the therapist under total control. The vulnerable time in treatment can be when this control begins to shift. In Ms Y's case, this was when the reality of her child's suffering began really to have an impact on her. As she and her son began to emerge from a state of confusion, she began to shift and allow herself to show some vulnerability; but this was a difficult time, and she had to be supported to stick with treatment, rather than run off or give up.

Working with all these types of families is very difficult, both for staff and for the patients themselves. As a therapist, one has to withstand a considerable amount of confusion, denigration and seduction. One can only see a limited number of such people, for the sake of one's own mental health. After all, there is the danger of becoming an abused therapist, who cannot then help the patient. It is no doubt important that, in order to help in these situations, the therapist needs to be understanding and empathic, but also open to feeling horror. The moment the therapist becomes blasé about what he or she is hearing is probably the moment either to take a holiday or to stop this sort of work.

8 PSYCHOSIS AND FAMILY TREATMENT:
Munchausen Syndrome by Proxy and Post-natal Breakdown

Psychotic phenomena occur in many of the families treated at the Cassel. There has been some mention in other chapters of how some families may use psychotic processes, such as severe projection, merging and splitting. This chapter will focus specifically on psychotic processes, using the clinical picture presented in Munchausen syndrome by proxy and severe post-natal breakdown to illustrate relevant points. In the treatment of both these conditions, it can be important to take account of psychotic processes in order both to keep the children safe and to promote change.

Although the Cassel rarely has acutely psychotic patients, we have had families in which one member has been manic-depressive, and some limited experience in working with schizophrenic parents, one of whom was discussed in Chapter 2. Though we may not treat much acute psychosis, a psychoanalytic approach to the handling of psychotic phenomena of various kinds, some of a very worrying and serious nature, is crucial to the treatment programme. Indeed, one could even go so far as to suggest that it is due to the psychoanalytical understanding of psychotic phenomena that we can attempt to take on such difficult families, whom others have often despaired of treating even though they may felt it worthwhile to try. An additional therapeutic factor is that we aim to provide a framework to help staff deal with the stresses and strains such work provokes in them. This can be done by looking in detail at transference and countertransference issues, as well as helping staff to work with and tolerate a certain amount of psychotic transference phenomena, often of a very destructive kind.

There follows a discussion of some general points about Psychosis, before moving on to a more detailed description of the clinical conditions.

PSYCHOTIC ANXIETY, PSYCHOTIC FUNCTIONING AND PSYCHOTIC BREAKDOWN

In psychoanalysis, the term psychosis is, of course, used rather loosely and is not limited to specific conditions along the lines of the medical model of mental disturbance. People these days talk of psychotic states of varying degrees of severity. Patients may spend limited or extended periods of time in such states. Patients may reveal what is going on in their minds; but not infrequently one may have to guess about what is going on, or make inferences from manifest behaviour. Some patients are adept at concealing psychotic processes, for a variety of reasons, such as fear of the consequences to their treatment or concern that the professional may be unable to bear the emotional strain involved in tolerating psychotic states.

In analysis, when one talks about psychosis a number of words come to mind which cover the field. First, there is the use of primitive defence mechanisms, which may or may not be synonymous with developmentally early defence mechanisms. Second, there are a number of negative descriptions associated with the term. These include loss of function or breakdown in functioning, collapse of the ego's defences and/or functioning, withdrawal from the social world, a disturbance in the reality sense, loose ego boundaries, severe communication problems, severe relationship difficulties, a terror of relatedness and the sense of some inner catastrophe. There is a quality of acute anxiety and of being despairingly alone and in the grip of some terrifying and maddening thoughts, of a sexual or other kind.

Rather than a model of individual disease categories, one can use a notion of three descriptive (not aetiological) categories, which seem to cover most of this confusing field of psychotic states: psychotic anxieties, psychotic functioning and psychotic breakdown.

Psychotic Anxieties are universal. Anyone who has been in a large group, or who has treated ill families, can testify to this. For example, in the large group projective processes are widespread, there is the attempt to rid oneself of unwanted thoughts and feelings by assigning them to others or requiring, in an intense way, others to experience them. The individual's own sense of identity becomes loose, persecutory anxiety abounds as does a sense of feeling anonymous in the crowd. It is difficult to feel sane; easy to feel mad. In the treatment of individuals or families, psychotic anxieties may be seen in a number of ways. At moments when one may be approaching psychotic anxieties, the therapist may find him- or herself feeling confused, unable to think, aware of fears about falling apart, in touch with an omnipotent denial of others, in touch with a push towards merging with the other and the blurring of personal boundaries. There may also be anxieties about the therapist's sanity. Some families are particularly prone to flipping into such anxious states when under stress. Their children may become particularly vulnerable to abuse or neglect at such moments. The kinds of issues which particularly seem to evoke psychotic anxieties in these families include issues of dependency, closeness and intimacy.

Psychotic Functioning refers to a more serious state of affairs not only when one or more people are expressing psychotic anxieties, but also when there is a major disturbance in their relationship to the world. There may be brief episodes when the individuals lose touch with the world, or with their children; they may have delusional ideas about themselves, their bodies or their children, for brief or extended periods of time. In psychosis, there is an attempt to remodel reality; to impose a view on others which may be unamenable to discussion. Social services may become the source of all badness; the parents the supposedly innocent victims of the authorities, despite the parents having abused their child. Injuries to a child may be seen as only 'accidental' and not the result of the parents' violent attacks; that is, to apply Bion's thought, there is an attack on linking of experiences (Bion, 1959).

Workers, when dealing with such situations in the child-care field, may be forced to act, to provide a less delusional reality for a child. In treatment situations, it may be equally important to resist acting too soon. Treatment of individuals and families who show psychotic functioning is bound to be very difficult, involving periods of risk and conflict between staff and authorities. Often there are intense feelings of disappointment and failed hopes and expectations among both staff and patients when the psychotic core of illness of the patient is really touched. At such times it is important to help staff maintain a sense of separateness while they are simultaneously dealing with the powerful projections, and so on, coming from the patients. Also at these times, staff may be taken over by unrealistic wishes to cure the patients, so that the staff can go on and on attempting the impossible, and thus making the patients worse.

One may ask, when does psychotic functioning tip over into Psychotic breakdown? Breakdown refers to the situation when the ego, either in the individual or in the family group (the 'family ego') can no longer hold the personality, or the family structure, together. There may be a severe suicide attempt, or delusional ideas may overwhelm the personality or the family field. Projective systems in the family may be so persistent and intense that the family's whole pattern of living becomes unstable, and the bricks and mortar of the family home fall apart.

Breakdown is, of course, a very loose term. Winnicott (1974) used it to describe 'The unthinkable state of affairs that underlies the defensive organization.' It seems to involve both external signs that something is wrong, and a view of the subject's inner experience of bewilderment and chaos. A form of hatred also seems to become evident. On the one hand, there is the apparent hatred of reality, the distortions in ego functioning, and so on, but, on the other hand, there is also a hatred for unreality. That is, there is also an attempt, however desperate, to relate, to repair damage. It also seems to be important in this context to recognize idealization of destructive parts of the self (see Rosenfeld, 1987).

As far as the complex issue of the aetiology of psychotic states in these families is concerned, one could emphasize the crucial role of disturbed early mother–child relationships – for example, over-symbiotic interactions and projective systems – for future psychotic developments. The father's role as the 'third party', offering a different structure from that provided by the mother and hence a potential way out of the psychotic situation, is no doubt also of relevance here.

In order to be able to treat families where there is a certain amount of psychotic functioning, leading occasionally to actual breakdown, one could suggest the need for a number of basic elements.

First of all, a setting with therapeutic structures for patients and supervision structures for staff, so that psychotic phenomena can be registered rather than fly around wildly, making everyone anxious and/or confused the whole time. A certain amount of confusion is inevitable, but not so much that the therapeutic environment goes into overload. It may be important in this context to have built-in safety structures, areas of the setting where patients can function away from the heat of the transference. That is, there is a need to provide next for the patient's ego strength, by interpreting the transference and also by taking account of the nature of the ego, its defences and fragility. Building up of ego strength through interpretative and non-interpretative means is vital in this work. In short, one needs a basic framework for treatment before embarking on interpretation.

Second, regression is inevitable in in-patient treatment, so it has to be monitored carefully. A certain amount of regression is useful as it enables a reworking of past conflicts to take place. But too much malignant regression (see Balint, M. 1968) can be very destructive. It can be difficult to know when to stop treating, when to say enough is enough, particularly when staff have put massive amounts of time and effort into a family. But one needs to have a realistic view of what can and cannot be achieved in therapy. For our work, the safety of the children and their welfare is the main reality that guides the treatment process. If at any time the children are seriously at risk, treatment will be ended, regardless of staff sympathies.

Finally, one needs to be able to support staff through the inevitable stresses and strains of this often arduous work. Not only is it immensely stressful to have to bear primitive anxieties and stand in the way of powerful destructive forces, but it is also stressful to have to give up treatment after all the input into the family.

POST-NATAL BREAKDOWN

Family work at the Cassel Hospital began in the 1950s with the treatment of post-natal breakdown, though only the mother was admitted at that time. Since the 1960s, fathers have also been admitted. In order to understand post-natal breakdown, it may help first of all to have a view of normal pregnancy.

The birth of a baby is obviously a major life event, a powerful developmental stage in the life of a woman and in the family. It can be highly pleasurable while, at the same time, it can produce enormous anxiety in adults and children around the pregnant mother and the mother and baby. Primitive anxieties may be stirred up during the pregnancy, and then more powerfully after the birth of the child, making women particularly vulnerable at this time. Mother and baby tend to be seen as a unit, as a natural partnership. While this is no doubt true, there are a considerable number of other figures around this unit, including husband, siblings, mothers, mothers-in-law – all of whom may have an interest in the birth and some of whom may help or interfere.

From the woman's point of view, there may be quite a difference between the wish to become pregnant and the wish to bring a live, new baby into the world. Probably the two wishes merge into one after the initial stages of pregnancy. A wish to be pregnant may be more to do with wanting to feel like a woman, without necessarily the added complication of a child. It may be, though not necessarily so, more about showing her own mother that she can produce a baby. At least at first, and perhaps nowadays until the first ultrasound, the new baby may feel unreal – an unseen and mysterious presence, which nonetheless has powerful emotional and physical effects on the mother. Indeed, during pregnancy one sees a complex interplay between body and mind, between bodily and emotional feelings, making it difficult to divide, in any meaningful way, these two aspects of the personality.

One of the main tasks for a new mother is the renegotiating of the mothering she herself had. If this was good enough, she will be able to tend to her baby and fulfil its needs. However, even in the normal mother, the turning back to the grandmother can produce considerable anxiety and confusion. In the early stages of pregnancy, the mother begins to feel merged bodily and emotionally in some way with the foetus. There is a strong identification with the foetus. Indeed, there is some evidence to show that the foetus may be affected by the mother's psychological state – it may be physically retained and given life, or rejected as in miscarriage when the mother may deny the foetus life and deny motherhood to herself.

It seems likely that once the first three months have passed, then a new phase of pregnancy begins. Awareness of the baby's movements, in particular, initiate a positive sense of the reality of the baby. Firmer psychological boundaries between mother and foetus begin to be established. A woman may begin to feel complete and whole. She becomes a new person. However, even in the normal mother, primitive anxieties are stirred up in ways that may not be repeated, and, indeed, may be completely forgotten later on. Such anxieties include fear of an abnormal or damaged baby; a fear about being able to cope with, or bond with, the baby, as well as worries that her own mother will interfere or criticize her, or find her wanting or inadequate. In the last phase of pregnancy there may be fears that her body will be permanently damaged, or that she will lose her husband's, or partner's love; that she will never become a sexual woman again.

After birth, if all goes reasonably well, the good enough mother becomes particularly focused around the baby. She and her partner have a strong and special emotional orientation to the baby. There is the capacity to identify what the baby needs for most of the time, and to allow the baby to be dependent.

This time is a developmental stage for both men and women in that both male and female sexuality usually develop in new ways. There were two; now there are three. Both partners have to adapt to a new way of life. Gone are the quick trips to the cinema and the lie-ins; instead, there is the terrifying responsibility of a new and highly vulnerable life. From the father's perspective, he may experience considerable anxieties about being displaced by the baby, especially after birth, when the mother is more interested in feeding the baby than in having sex. When things go well, as they usually do, both partners seem to be enveloped by an atmosphere of mutual excitement and preoccupation that overcomes rivalries and frustrations. There is also quite probably the important contribution of the personality of the baby in arousing the parents' responses. Some babies are placid while others are wakeful, whatever the parents do. Some feed well; others have difficulties. There are no absolute rules about how a baby will develop. Things can go wrong when the parents cannot constantly be flexible and perceptive about changes in the baby's state of physical and emotional well-being. It may be difficult to know how much the capacity to monitor the baby's changing state is a function of the mother, the father, or the couple. One could see the mother and father as having interrelated and overlapping roles and functions, but with some definite areas of difference, such as when the mother is breast-feeding.

If there are other young children in the family, then clearly the situation is rather more complicated. The most obvious thing is that siblings become intensely curious about the new baby and/or become intensely jealous, particularly when time and attention are given over to the baby. It may be more difficult when there is only a short gap between children, and when the older child cannot yet speak, and thus cannot yet put powerful jealous feelings into words.

This description of the birth of a normal baby could be seen to lay the basis for understanding what can go wrong. While for most women the psychological changes in pregnancy – of coming closer to her own mother, and of becoming identified with the foetus and then the baby – are pleasurable, for some women motherhood may be a painful and frightening experience. The turning back to the grandmother that occurs, and the identification with the foetus and then the baby, can become major threats to the woman's mental health if there were severe problems in her own mothering. Instead of turning back to her own mother, she may turn too much to the baby for comfort. She may not be able to differentiate herself from the baby; she may feel irrationally that her own mother disapproves of her. The three generations – grandmother, mother and baby – can become confused in her mind. The child and adult elements of the woman's personality may become confused. There is an identification with the baby, but, at the same time, a loss of the mothering capacity. The baby becomes the mother in a psychotic way. Also, the baby may come to represent the life-giver for the emotionally dead mother. This can be potentially dangerous, because the baby can also then become the target of other and more sinister projections. If there is, in addition, an absence of other support, for example, from the partner, then a woman may be tipped over into post-natal breakdown. This kind of usually borderline pathology is different from that of, say, schizophrenic mothers who may well have major problems looking after a baby.

In the Family Unit, treatment of post-natal depression consists of the following. Initially, a detailed nursing plan for a patient with a fragmented ego is drawn up, to contain anxiety and to provide support – this is because many women suffering from severe post-natal illness are in an acutely disturbed state, usually with psychotic functioning merging into breakdown. The nursing may include rotas of patients to help with the basic mothering tasks until she can take on more responsibility. Critical times such as bath times and feeding of the baby may become major focuses of nursing work. There are frequent mood changes, fluctuating between suicidal depression and manic denial of emotions. Because of this, it is important to remain vigilant throughout the first week or two of admission. Indeed, one of the most dangerous times is when the mother begins to feel less depressed. The problem may be that she then begins to feel very guilty about being ill and not attending to her baby. Staff may then begin to relax their attention and suicidal acts are more likely at this time.

We often also provide daily therapy sessions, sometimes of brief duration at first, as there is a need to monitor the situation from day to day. Gradually involving the father is vital. Not infrequently, they come across as having tried everything possible to help, and yet when one looks more closely there is a subtle attempt to put all the vulnerability and disturbance into the woman, with an attempt to extricate themselves from any responsibility for what has happened. Though the woman may collude with this state of affairs, it also results in her being overwhelmed by psychotic processes. There is no safe haven, and breakdown may ensue.

Clinical Example

A woman in her late thirties with a core identity problem, whom we have successfully treated recently, was admitted as her local services had poured in resources for her and her baby with minimal success. In fact, the baby, a few months old, was being looked after for half the week by professionals, at great financial cost to the social services. Her former partner had made it plain that he had wanted her to have an abortion, and when she decided to go through with the pregnancy he abandoned her and has had nothing further to do with her. Her own mother was hospitalized for severe depression when the patient was a teenager, and also suffered from depression when the patient was a child. Father was described as distant and unemotional. The patient had gone through periods of suicidal depression, but at other times was capable and held down a good job. She had a poor image of herself and was very sensitive to criticism. The nursing work focused on her mothering through looking at basic mothering activities. Though in part a capable mother, she had little awareness of the effect of her mood on her child. He was one of those children who somehow learn to cheer up their mothers, whereas other babies may become depressed and morose themselves. In therapeutic situations, mother tended to identify with staff and made helpful suggestions to other patients, but she had difficulty in focusing on herself. In individual therapy sessions, much of the early work was focused on quite subtle shifts in the transference, when she quickly tried to avoid feelings of dependency by becoming the therapist; partly to avoid being taken over by overwhelming feelings of loss of control, of psychotic intensity. The issue of how she covered up her anger but was seething underneath gradually became more amenable to treatment. Considerable work was done by one of the child psychotherapists on the mother–child relationship, with the aim of protecting the child from his mother's vulnerable mood states.

Other cases may be admitted in an acute emergency, but postnatal depression is one of the few psychotherapeutic emergencies, sometimes necessitating admission on the day of the consultation.

MUNCHAUSEN SYNDROME BY PROXY

There has already been a brief description of a family with this label in Chapter 2. A full clinical account of one case from the Cassel is given in a paper by Coombe (1995). The Family Unit has now successfully rehabilitated three such cases and has assessed a few others. In the Munchausen family, a seemingly caring and concerned parent, usually the mother, brings her child to the doctor with fabricated symptoms or induced serious illnesses. In the families we have treated, in one case the mother caused a previous child to go into a coma by administering a common household substance; in another, the mother administered aspirin and paracetamol to her child, which made her ill and present with blood in the urine; while another put her own blood in the baby's nappy in order to present herself to the doctor. The mothers consistently and convincingly lied about what they were doing, until confronted with the medical evidence. Indeed, one mother managed to convince the ward that she was a medical student. In the two cases in which the father was present, the fathers themselves turned a blind eye to what was happening, and vigorously backed up their partners' stories. The children were eventually removed from their parents and placed in foster homes. One parent only escaped a custodial sentence by being admitted to the Cassel; two of the mothers had probation orders, and all families were likely to lose their children if rehabilitation had not been on offer. Our own findings revealed severe personality problems in the parents, both individually and in the marital relationships. The mothers were self-centred and liked to control both their emotions and other people. All the mothers had major anxieties about their bodies; two of them were keen to have hysterectomies despite being young. Some workers in the hospital, as in other settings, were convinced of their dangerousness, while others could only believe in their good intentions – evidence of splitting processes. Two of the mothers were abused as children. In one mother, her sexual abuse was only revealed on admission to the Cassel. One father had a history of severe physical and sexual abuse as a child, which was also only uncovered on admission to the Cassel. Both of the couples revealed marital difficulties which seemed to contribute to the presenting symptoms. They had difficulty in communicating between themselves and instead used the child as a conduit for communication. The parents were also confused as to what should be said in public and what was private; they had sexual problems and difficulties in being intimate with one another.

There were major disturbances in the mother–child relationships. Although often saying the right things about their children, the mothers were in reality emotionally cold and distant, with little capacity to empathize with their children. They had difficulty in playing spontaneously with their children, whom they saw very often as mere extensions of themselves, to be used as they saw fit. At times, the children were seen as objects to be used by the mothers for mere comfort for themselves. The mothers who completed the treatment programme revealed powerful and primitive aggressive fantasies, centred around both their own bodies and their children, possibly related to their own childhood experiences of being abused. At times they were close to collapse and disintegration, and needed considerable amounts of help and support of the kind which seems able to be provided only in an in-patient setting.

Treatment was prolonged in two of these cases, requiring nearly two years before the families were considered safe enough to return to their communities. Regular and then random monitoring of urine specimens was maintained for much of the admission. Crucial to change was the capacity of the parents, particularly the mothers, both to face their own destructive feelings and to experience feelings of dependency, towards both staff and other people, without collapsing. These changes enabled them to be more in touch with their children and to show for the first time appropriate concern for them. The children themselves also had individual therapy, which helped them to make sense of their experience and to become less emotionally disturbed.

Clinical Example

The family consisted of father, in his thirties, and mother, in her twenties, and a four-year-old boy, whom the mother had poisoned with analgesics. Mother's parents divorced when she was young. Her stepfather physically abused her, while there was little emotional rapport with her mother. Father, at first, denied problems and described his childhood as happy but, on admission, revealed that as a child he had been subjected to severe and repeated sadistic sexual abuse. The marital relationship was very confused at assessment. Though living in the same house, they led separate lives. Thus, when the poisoning began, the father could plead ignorance. A major problem for both parents was a fear of closeness and expression of intimacy. It became clear how much both of them were still involved with one another, though apparently living apart. Their child showed severe emotional and learning problems that required both intensive psychotherapy and remedial help in the hospital's school.

The treatment was difficult and at times anxiety provoking. Once they decided to try to work together as a couple, staff could see how furious they were with one another, but they themselves could barely acknowledge this. Their child was used by them as a kind of spokesperson, saying to each what the other could not say. Mother revealed intense jealousy of her child, barely allowing him any separate space; and she could hardly play with him. Father often maintained an impenetrable attitude of denying problems, while getting into quarrels with authority figures.

Despite their difficulties, the parents made significant changes. Father became more assertive and less defensive, while mother was more able to face her own aggressive feelings without involving the child and showed more appropriate concern for him. On discharge, their child had begun attending a normal school.

Treatment of these cases is clearly difficult and at times anxiety provoking. Indeed, when workers stop feeling anxious about them, then there may be a dangerous risk of complacency. There is still much we do not understand about the syndrome. Though we have only treated three cases in depth, what seemed to be essential in those cases, both in diagnosis and in treatment, was the quality of the mother–child relationship. Essentially, the mother attacks her child, or gets others to attack it, in order to find care from the medical profession. The child comes first of all to represent in a psychotic way the unwanted parts of the mother, the aspects she wishes to attack – particularly the dependent aspects. These mothers hate recognizing dependency in themselves, so it is not surprising if their dependent children are subjected to forms of violence. But the child also represents another, more hopeful side in however patho-logical a form, in that there is a turning towards a professional for care and concern. The situation can be more complicated when in-volving a couple, for the attack on the child may in part be aimed at the impervious partner. The child is used as a pawn in their marital conflict.

As already described, the mothers have great difficulty in acknowledging their own aggressive impulses. Like the doctors who see them at first, they themselves cannot believe how poi-soning and destructive they can be. As a result, workers are often left to experience the anxiety about the child. However, in the families we treated, tackling the mother's aggression was a crucial element of treatment and helped to enable the mothers to allow their children to be more separate from them. But it must be said that tackling the aggression and going into the details of the mother's often primitive and violent psychotic fantasies re-quires a fair amount of psychotherapeutic skill. The mothers were treated by experienced therapists and in a treatment setting supervised by an experienced clinician. Such work may not be possible in other less intensive and less established settings.

Finally, in the families that were treated, sexual and physical abuse was an important element of the family history. Though by no means a universal finding in this syndrome, one suspects that it must have had an important part to play in determining the quality of parenting in these cases.

9 THE ABUSED CHILD, THE ABUSED ADULT AND RECOVERED MEMORIES OF ABUSE

This chapter puts together a number of observations about the abused children in the families we treat and their parents. In addition, the issue of memories of abuse recovered in psychoanalytic treatment of adults is addressed, based on the author's practice as a psychoanalyst. This is currently a controversial issue, and for this reason, there is an attempt to offer a balanced view of the issue of recovered memories based on having seen many families where the evidence for abuse has been undisputed and very often confirmed by a Court of Law.

WORKING WITH THE ABUSED MIND

There will be an attempt to look at the nature of the abused mind, the nature of the memories of abuse and the way that the abusing experience may be repeated in psychoanalytic treatment by making an emotional impact of a particular kind on the analyst.

Most psychoanalytic theories of development emphasize the need for the young child to be able to have an early experience of safe dependence, safe physical and emotional boundaries around him or her, and help to be able to tolerate inevitable environmental frustrations. One may then ask, what happens to the mind's development when these conditions are not provided, when bodily boundaries are intruded upon and when primitive sexual desires are enacted in the real world? One could argue that there is still only the general outline of an answer to this unfortunate question. The abused mind seems to show varying degrees of damage and developmental distortion, depending on the nature of the abuse, the quality of family relationships and the resilience of the child. In later life, the abused adults inevitably bring with them feelings of abandonment, mistrust and parental failure, which are repeated in the analysis and in the Cassel treatment programme with varying degrees of intensity, depending on how the original trauma has been dealt with. Having been used as mere objects to satisfy primitive sexual and/or aggressive impulses in adults, they themselves in adult life show varying degrees of psychic damage, particularly in their capacity for self-reflection. By calling on observations from the two clinical fields of psychoanalysis and family treatment at the Cassel, it may be possible to bring to this difficult and, at times, controversial area of clinical concern, some reasonably sober issues for discussion.

Before tackling the subject in detail, one needs to emphasize the need to be cautious in making assertions about the status of memories of abuse. The diagnosis of abuse in children is a complex affair, involving detailed assessment of the child's report of abuse, combined with attention to the nature of the family pathology and the nature of any corroborative evidence, while recognizing the frequent presence of coercion of children by adults, with threats to the children if the abuse is revealed. Memories of abuse recovered in adult analysis cannot be subjected to the same clear procedures and are thus inevitably subject to considerable doubt. The analyst also needs to be wary of a kind of unconscious coercion on his or her part either to suggest abusing memories or to help to deny them. Thus it can be seen to be important that such recovered memories be subjected to a rigorous examination of their supposed reality by, for example, the analyst remaining initially sceptical, or at least open-minded, about their reality; by assessing the nature of other memories of the past, as well as the quality of the transference at the time of their recall; and by the analyst exercising caution in accepting the reality of the abuse, however convincing it may appear at first.

It is worth noting in this context that in Freud's early paper on the aetiology of hysteria (1896, p. 205) he draws up comprehensive criteria for assessing the reality of infantile sexual scenes. These criteria include the uniformity which they exhibit in certain details; the initial insignificance which the patient first of all ascribes to the events, despite their horrifying consequences; the way the patient does not put particular stress on the events; and, finally, the relationship of the scenes to the content of the whole of the rest of the case history. He compares the unravelling of the early scenes of seduction to the putting together of a child's picture puzzle. Having subjected the memories to a rigorous examination, it may then be possible to accept the abuse as having actually happened. Indeed, it may be very important, for clinical and human reasons, for the patient to feel that the analyst has understood that there has been real abuse in the patient's past, that it can be dealt with and talked about, but that one does not necessarily have to accept that the abuse explains everything. One cannot of course expect absolute certainty in this area, for the evidence involved in the analytic process is not of the kind involved in the natural sciences, but more like that involved in the social and legal field, where life has to be lived and decisions made on everyday criteria. Thus, if natural science evidence were used in cases of child abuse, probably no child would be protected from an abuser. Freud began by believing that hysteria was primarily caused by the sexual molestation of children. As is well known, he then felt that he had overvalued reality and undervalued fantasy (1896, p. 204). It may be important that we over-value neither reality nor fantasy, but accept that there is a complex interweaving of both fantasy and reality in the processes of memory. Though this interweaving process may complicate judgements about the reality of past events, it also provides for the richness and complexity of the analytic task, and makes it particularly well suited to explore the nature of memory.

Freud himself, in his early paper on hysteria, outlines a complex picture of the nature of memory. Thus, he emphasizes that it is not the original trauma of seduction itself that causes subsequent hysterical symptoms, but their reproduction in symbolic form in unconscious memories.

Our view then is that infantile sexual experiences are the fundamental precondition for hysteria, are, as it were, the *disposition* for it and that it is they which create the hysterical symptoms, but that they do not do so immediately, but remain without effect to begin with and only exercise a pathogenic action later, when they have been aroused after puberty in the form of unconscious memories. (1896, p. 212)

The trauma thus acquires new meaning by 'deferred action' or 'after revision', by rearrangement of memory traces. Of course, it is now known that in addition to the delayed effect of sexual trauma on the adult, the child may also be directly and immediately affected by abuse, sometimes with very damaging and long-lasting results. Presumably, the population seen by Freud was not so totally damaged by any abuse, as is perhaps still the case for those now in analysis.

Freud's emphasis on the role of the arrival of genital maturity at puberty as the extra factor needed to create symptomatology is matched by experiences at the Cassel Hospital with young abusing adults, most of whom have themselves been abused as children. Many of the abusing parents left home early as a result of conflict with their parents, and had a stormy adolescence, with episodes of acute depression. Several parents had promiscuous sexual relations at that time; others attempted to deal with their adolescent problems by a premature first marriage or equivalent, which soon broke down. One has the impression that there was often a threat of an adolescent breakdown, perhaps related to the flooding back of conscious or unconscious memories of abuse, which was warded off unsatisfactorily by various environmental premature and false solutions.

Jacques Lacan (1966), in particular, has drawn attention to the importance in early and later Freud of memories which have been subjected to after revision, or *Nachträglichkeint*. The philosopher Jacques Derrida (1967) has also used Freud's concept in his particular emphasis in his thought on the place of memory traces. Both Lacan and Derrida point out that as early as in the Freud–Fliess letters, (6 December 1896) Freud speculates on the nature of memory.

As you know, I am working on the assumption that our psychic mechanism has come into being by a process of stratification: the material present in the form of memory traces being subjected from time to time to a *rearrangement* in accordance with fresh circumstances – to a *retranscription*.

In the early paper on hysteria, Freud writes of the 'posthumous' effects after puberty of memory which produced symptoms, rather than merely the effect of the original trauma (1896, p. 213). However, one could perhaps wonder whether or not there are certain early experiences, for example, where there has been massive and repeated abuse, that remain constantly pathogenic, with rather little rearrangement in the memory. Indeed, contemporary child development research (see, for example, Goldwyn and Main, 1997) has shown that there are clear continuities in experiences, patterns of behaviour and narrative styles that continue from infancy to later childhood. For example, securely attached infants subsequently, aged six and eleven, make good coherent narratives about issues of separation. Their early attachment pattern is highly predictive of their subsequent narrative capacities. Similarly, insecurely attached infants subsequently produce insecure and more disorganized narratives. One may also wonder which kinds of experience show such clear continuities over time, with little rearrangement, and what kinds of experience show discontinuities with varying degrees of rearrangement and distortion.

THE ABUSED CHILD

Before presenting some clinical material from an adult patient, it may be useful to bring together some thoughts and observations about the effect of child abuse on children, from the Cassel setting, in order to provide a backdrop to the more traditional psychoanalytic work. There is now considerable evidence from clinical and research findings (see, for example, Bentovim et al., 1988) to show that the effect of sexual abuse, usually involving genital and/or anal penetration, has lasting effects on the child's developing mind and personality, including the production of wide-ranging behavioural, emotional and learning difficulties. Psychosomatic symptoms, over-preoccupation with sexual matters, inappropriate sexual behaviour and aggressive behaviour can occur in those severely and persistently abused. In adolescence, sexual abuse can be associated with anorexia, attempted suicide, self-harm, prostitution and long-term depression. Increasing evidence of previously undisclosed sexual abuse is being discovered in the population of psychiatric patients. I have seen several women who seemed normal until the birth of their first child, when memories of their own child abuse has suddenly flooded them once they were faced with the reality of their own vulnerable child. It can be quite difficult to define what is specific to the effect of abuse on the child and subsequent adult in these situations; but what seems to stand out is that the victims of abuse vary greatly in the way that they handle the trauma, depending on the severity of the abuse, the nature of the family relationships at the time, the temperaments of the children, and their capacity for resilience. The abuse can be dealt with reasonably effectively, or it can be encapsulated or compartmentalized within the person's mind, with varying subsequent effects, or it can have a massively damaging effect on many aspects of the personality. The latter situation tends to be seen in the population admitted to the Cassel Hospital, with less global damage in those seen in psychoanalytic practice. However, what is common, though perhaps obvious, to all these abusing situations, is that not only has the child's body been used and abused as a mere object by another (usually an adult, but sometimes another child), but that the child's mind is also affected, and may have great difficulty in being able to function effectively. Quite how it is affected may well vary greatly, and we still know little about what happens. Learning problems, with impairment in the capacity for symbolic thought, are common. Formal research at the Cassel on the abusing parents who have abused their children has so far shown that often on admission they reveal great difficulties in their capacity to reflect on their past and present experiences. Those parents who improve during treatment show a changed capacity for self-reflection and this seems matched by their improved relationships with their children. Clearly, then, the abuse has major effects on the capacity of the mind to remember the past and to make emotional sense of experiences.

It would seem that what can be damaging is the merging of the damaged adult's mind with the vulnerable and immature child's mind, where there has been an active intrusion into the child's bodily and mental boundaries. Laplanche (1987) has emphasized that there is always a seduction by the adult of the child, as the child is relatively helpless and immature at first and has to confront the adult's mind. His notion of a primary seduction has, however, nothing to do with a sexual assault. Primary seduction describes a situation 'in which an adult proffers to a child verbal, non-verbal and even behavioural signifiers which are pregnant with unconscious sexual signification' (p. 126).

Though the child is, of course, immature, nonetheless the kind of evidence now coming from child development research (see, for example, Stern, 1985) shows that infants are in many ways exquisitely adapted to their situation, that of actively and even creatively eliciting care from the parent. Babies are very active, aware of their surroundings, and constantly making sophisticated discriminations about their caretakers. They even seem to learn through their emotions and through their relationships. Learning takes place through shared affect in the context of a relationship, one in which the baby is not some passive and helpless partner. For example, experiments closely observing mother–baby interactions show that the baby's reactions are imitated by the mother, as much as the baby imitates her. That is, the baby conveys meanings to the mother as much as the mother conveys meanings to the baby.

However, Laplanche emphasizes how the adult unconsciously conveys sexual meanings, which the baby cannot yet adequately comprehend and, in this sense, there is seduction. Presumably, if there is then an actual seduction of the growing child, then there is damage to the quality of the child's subsequent relating, and an impairment in the capacity to deal with the signifying environment.

The children at the Cassel Hospital often seem haunted by their abuse and unable to free themselves from its consequences without considerable help. As others have repeatedly observed, such children often show a number of pathological features. For example, they may be unable to concentrate on a task for long; appear over-stimulated with poor impulse control; have a haunted and driven quality in their relating and a tendency to be aggressive and testing of boundaries; they sometimes show inappropriate sexual behaviour; they may go in and out of confusional states when they become very anxious, particularly about being abandoned; they have difficulty in trusting adults; and, in more ordinary terms, they can be very intrusive and irritating in their behaviour. The parent–child relationships are usually pathological, with varying degrees of disorganized attachment patterns. There is often role reversal, in which the children try to control the parent and are over-solicitous, while the parents have problems in maintaining ordinary child–adult boundaries. The children may have a build-up of emotional tension with which the parent cannot deal, which then leads to an outburst of frustration and despair. These episodes may be accompanied by the projection of primitive fantasies between child and adult, in which there is a mix-up of child and adult elements. The children may be confused about their own identity and also trying to expel the 'malignant' projections coming from the adult. This kind of repetition may be evidence of an earlier failure to help the children build up integrating experiences.

A frequent simple finding in the parents is that they consistently show great difficulty in being emotionally attached to their children, with inhibition of the capacity to play. They are often inconsistent, at times cut off and self-absorbed. Suicidal feelings in them may be triggered off by the threat of experiencing vulnerability. Acting rather than understanding is a common means of communicating for both parents and children, which often makes the treatment of both very demanding and at times exhausting. This is particularly the case when the staff may have to be the ones who feel the child's pain and vulnerability for the parent. There often seems to be a need for the children to make a particular kind of powerful emotional impact on their parents and other caretakers, especially when the parents are impervious to the child's emotional needs. The children may be trying desperately to get the parents to acknowledge their needs, while also attacking them for having failed them. Many of these children have had to suffer in solitude, and have had to bear, on their own, horrific experiences.

THE ABUSED ADULT

It may be unlikely that a severely abused child will end up in later life in psychoanalysis, as desirable as it may be for them to have such help. The abused adults one tends to see in analysis have somehow managed to wall off their traumatic experiences to a greater or lesser extent, though these experiences usually remain essentially unresolved. This is not to underplay the horrors of their own experience; but they have tended either to be particularly resilient personalities, and/or to have had some reasonably good early lcaretaking. One may wonder, what is the effect on the mind to have to keep such experiences walled off or hermetically sealed? One consequence may well be that certain 'imaginative' elements of mental life, such as dreams and fantasy life, may also have a sealed off and unavailable quality to them. These elements may be felt as persecuting or as almost inanimate objects, split off from the rest of the mind.

Research at the Cassel Hospital has, so far, indicated that adults who have had abusing experiences in childhood and who respond to these experiences by an inhibition of reflective self-function are less likely to resolve their abuse, and are also more likely to manifest borderline pathology (Fonagy et al., 1996). Their diminished capacity for self-reflection seems to make them unlikely to seek the kind of self-reflective help offered by psychoanalysis; instead, they will look for environmental solutions to their difficulties. From the effect of our treatment programme, the indications are that if the abused child or adult has access to a relationship which can help them deal with the emotional impact of their abuse, they can to some degree resolve the experience; they may then be protected from severe borderline pathology.

In a sense, the treatment experience provides a setting for the possibility of just such a resolution of past abuse. Indeed, the treatment of the abused child is perhaps less concerned with the issue of recovered memories of the past as such than in confronting the emotional impact of the abuse, and the effect of the abuse on the mind's emotional functioning. Not infrequently, this issue arrives in

an analysis when the patient makes a particular kind of em.
impact on the analyst. It would be too simplistic to descri
situation as being one in which the analyst becomes the abuser i
transference; though not untrue, it seems too gross a description of
what may take place. Rather, the analyst almost inevitably proves to
be a failure; there is a breakdown in usual functioning; a failure of
nerve or some lapse in concentration. The reasonably empathic
atmosphere may suddenly deteriorate, with the ready creation of
misunderstandings, which may leave the analyst feeling that he or
she has somehow mistreated the patient. Rather as in the treatment
of abused children outlined above, the abused adult will re-create the
emotionally absent parent, the parent who could not bear the child's
pain and vulnerability and who has left the child with a sense that
the environment has fundamentally failed him or her, and that there
is a kind of breach, or unbridgeable gap, in the parenting experience.
An unbridgeable gulf may suddenly appear between patient and
analyst, which either party may be tempted to deal with by some
kind of precipitous action, such as termination. Bearing the
unbearable is an issue in any analysis, but with the abused adult it
somehow becomes acutely relevant. Other themes may include the
familiar one of testing of the analytic boundaries and over-
emphasizing the role of the abuse, by, for example, tapping into the
analyst's wish to find answers rather than accept uncertainty. Finally,
the pre-abused child's body may become idealized, while the post-
abused body may become a source of persecution. The patient's body,
which obviously experienced real intrusion and damage, may feel
unintegrated.

Clinical Example

The following is a selection of some disguised clinical material
from a thirty-year-old woman in analysis, who had experienced
sexual abuse as a child by an uncle. The memories of abuse
were repressed until quite early on in the analysis, when she got
into a difficult work relationship. She would constantly complain
about a man at work who was mistreating her, and so on. This
was someone on whom she had pinned great hopes, and his
treatment of her was a great disappointment to her. Of course,
at first, I assumed this was all very relevant transference material, and took it up in this way. However, my doing so made
little difference to her sense of being misused and, in her own
words, abused. From what I knew of her family background,
there were indications of some parental failure. She had had

some basic good experiences, but the parents tended to leave her and her sibling in the care of relatives from time to time. The fact that she was left in my care in the analysis, that she felt abused at work, that she had a certain amount of difficulty in dealing with fantasy and dreams, that she was also rather controlling of me in sessions, and that there had been significant gaps in her parenting, made me suspect some kind of childhood abuse. Eventually, and rather tentatively, I wondered with her if she had actually been molested in some way as a child. My question produced some relief and, soon after, memories of sexual abuse by an uncle, which she had kept to herself as a child and then forgotten. Her sense of grievance towards the work figure retreated. I should also add that she has never wanted to seek revenge either on her uncle or her parents for what had happened, as has been the case with some patients undergoing various kinds of therapy. Nor has the abuse become the major focus of the analysis. There are many other issues; but it does remain highly significant as an event around which so much of her emotional life crystallized; and I am convinced, after careful consideration, that it actually occurred.

After her recall of abuse, I became rather idealized for a while in the analysis for having understood her. It took some time before she could really show her disappointment with me. But breaks were very difficult, with intense feelings of loss and abandonment. There were for a time very fragmented sessions, with intense psychotic anxieties predominating. I then seemed to become the detached mother, unable to relate affectively to the child; the mother who could not pick up that she was going to leave her child in unsafe hands in her absence. For obvious reasons of confidentiality, it would not be appropriate to set out too much more of her history; but I shall instead present part of a session which I think highlights some of the issues around her need to make an emotional impact on me.

The background to this session, a month or so before a Christmas break, was that I had had to change the previous day's session time, several weeks before. She was unusually and exceedingly furious with me.

She began with a dream. I had moved from my consulting room. The new place was attached to the American Embassy (America is often a reference to me, because of my name). She came to see me a little before time. She sat outside on a ledge, comfortably. I came out and said that she could not wait there. There was a fierce argument between us. I accused her of intruding. I was unreasonable and wanted her to go. She was disgusted and upset.

She soon became furious with me again, as she had to submit to me. She complained how patients have to adapt to analysts and not the other way around. I first of all said that perhaps she was furious with me for appearing to put myself first and not think about her and what she might feel about the session change.

Still with some fury and a sense of grievance, she said that what I said reminded her of how she had had to adapt to her parents; how they went off, leaving her in her uncle's unsafe care. She expressed a deep sense of grievance about what had been done to her. Also, she felt second class. She had had to be too responsible as a child, when she was not ready for it. I was struck by the feelings she described of being a helpless child and her attitude to the session change; and how she talked about having to be in my care on what she felt were my terms, not under her control. I said that it sounded that the session change had made her feel powerless about what had been done to her, and I added that she sounded afraid of what her anger might have done to me (the issue of her intruding also came into the session around this point).

This led to various childhood memories, centred around the theme of how her parents could not tolerate her anger. I took up the feelings of despair that she had not been allowed to have, that had arisen around the session change and which she was able to show me. Later, we touched on the way that she felt we were no longer in touch when she had felt that I had thrown her out and abandoned her. The issue of the coming Christmas break was also touched upon.

The subsequent session highlighted how her mother had had difficulties tolerating signs of protest from my patient – perhaps part of the reason why my patient had kept the abuse to herself. This issue had left my patient with difficulties in being able to tolerate dependency in herself and those close to her. She tended to use control to fend off feelings of chaos when she became intimate with another person. She was also surprised that she could be so angry with me and yet fond of me. This mixture of feelings was a new experience for her. I did feel that something quite important had taken place, in that an essential element in the parenting failure, which had allowed the abuse to take place and to be kept secret, had been repeated in the transference to me, providing the opportunity for some working through of the trauma.

In this example, my patient tried to provoke me with her fury. I had to restrain myself from getting into an argument, or from trying to persuade her that she was being unreasonable in being so angry about a fairly minor session change, one which had been anticipated some weeks before. Her unusually fierce anger had certainly made its impact in the session prior to the one I reported. I had been unable to say very much. I was just aware of needing to hold on and not be provoked too much. I did spend some time after that session wondering what it was about, which helped me cope when I saw her again. I think a major anxiety in the session was a fear of abandonment. She had to make an impact on me about this issue, and I had to feel the full brunt of her fury. Failure to do so, including perhaps too premature an interpretation of it, might have resulted in a different kind of failure, which would not have addressed the central issue of the way she had never been allowed to have her emotions, or the way they had not been suitably registered and tolerated. The trauma of abuse, with bodily intrusion, had taken place in a particular emotional context, and it was this context which was important to clarify as much as the actual abuse itself. Of course, my patient is a long way from the severely abused children I have described above. For all their failings, her parents seemed also loving and concerned about her. However, one can see common ground in, for example, the issue of bearing intolerable feelings to do with abandonment and fears of intrusion. Certainly in our work with severely abusing families at the Cassel Hospital, these are common issues in treatment.

There is also the common issue of the attack on the vulnerable and dependent child. Destructive attacks on children can, unfortunately, have quite specific meaning for the adult perpetrator. The abused child, at a particular moment of vulnerability – for example, when showing acute signs of distress or helplessness, or signs of temper and separateness from the parents' control – can suddenly be experienced by the parent as an enormous threat. The psychic pain shown by the helpless or out of control child cannot be tolerated by the abusing parent. In severe cases, the child can be seen as all-destructive and as taking away the parent's goodness. The parents cannot experience the pain of the helpless child as it poses too great a threat to the parent's self, which has great difficulty in being able to reflect on experiences.

There may also be a vengeful aspect to the attack, whether physical and/or sexual. The damage done to the child is a revenge for the psychic and physical damage done to the parents, or other perpetrator, when they themselves were children. The particular cruelty or malignancy sometimes shown by the abusing parents to their victims seems in part to be a result of the unconscious need to avenge the neglected child in themselves. Recent reports of adults in dubious therapies who want actual revenge on their parents may be the result of their being caught up in this particular dynamic.

Treatment of the severely abused adult may involve having to deal with various 'abuse equivalents'. There is repetition in the transference of the kind of parental care system around the child which led to the abuse. The abused child has been subjected to significant impingements, with breaks in the provision of continuous care. These gaps in the holding structure may be small enough to be glossed over, or to be kept just about intact by some kind of temporary repair. Or they may be so great as to cause major psychic damage, with borderline pathology. In treatment, the analyst may be seen as part of a constantly failing environment. There may also be a wish to keep the analyst under total control, for example, through the fantasy of merging. The analyst may experience abuse of his or her own mind by the patient's wish to merge with it and to take it over. Any sign of independence shown by the analyst, for example, by making interpretations, may be sorely resented by the patient; which again makes treatment of the severely abused adult very difficult.

Finally, to return to the status of recovered memories in analysis, one may need to look at the nature of the narratives with which the analyst deals. Freud, in 'Moses and Monotheism' (1939, p. 129), distinguishes between material and historical truth. There is the material truth of what happened in the past, which we may never know for certain in all its details. We are presented in time with distortions about what happened, that is, with historical truth, but we are still able to reconstruct what may have happened, at least in outline. But in addition, Freud's theory of memory as a constant rearrangement in the light of subsequent events implies that, with time, the past is always rearranged. Material truth is no longer of central concern to analysts; instead, they are concerned with what the person has made of the past. History itself is a constant rearrangement. Once one look backs, one has altered history, or begun to create it or rewrite it. It is the story itself that is of interest, not so much what began the story.

One could also have the view that analysis deals with what one could call 'relational truth', that is, the truth of what becomes repeated in the transference, in the specific ways the patient relates to the analyst, is the truth with which the analyst can deal. Anything else in the end is speculation. Relational truth is a mixture of material and historical elements, together with a particular narrative style unique to the individual's relationship with the analyst, added to the way the patient relates. However, this view does not underestimate the way that actual experiences of abuse can, and indeed should, make a powerful emotional impact on the analyst. The abusing narrative has its own truth to tell.

10 FAMILY LAW ISSUES

This final chapter will tackle some of the issues that have arisen as a result of the Cassel's work with family lawyers, both when members of staff have been giving evidence in court and when they have had discussions with senior family judges. It is perhaps worth mentioning first of all that on 28 November 1996 the House of Lords made a landmark decision when it ruled that a court has the power to order a local authority to pay for a residential assessment. This followed from a case in which a local judge had ordered such an assessment which the local authority was unwilling to fund, mainly on financial grounds. The Court of Appeal rather reluctantly ruled against the judge, but the House of Lords overturned the appeal. They considered that before a child should be removed permanently from the parents, the court needed to have full information about the family's capacities, and that the local authority could not usurp the court's function by refusing to fund a residential assessment. This judgment will obviously have a major impact on the Cassel's work; it is hoped that it will open up the Cassel's resources to families who otherwise would not have found backing from their local services purely on narrow short-term financial grounds.

Actually appearing in court can be a time consuming and sometimes frustrating business. In fact, we usually only have to give evidence in situations where we have recommended removal of children from their parents or when there is a contested hearing. It is relatively rare to attend when we have positive recommendations and when rehabilitation is succeeding. However, we are usually involved in meetings with workers around a family in preparation for a court hearing (*see also* King and Trowell, 1992).

Such meetings have a variety of purposes, depending on the issues involved in a particular family. If the opinions of various experts are very different, then a meeting can be useful in order to make clear for the court areas of agreement and disagreement. This can obviously save a considerable amount of court time. However, it may be very difficult indeed for experts to meet together, unless the judge in the case has specifically ordered it, and even then, it is not uncommon for at least one of the experts to suddenly not appear at the last moment, which may or may not reflect the family's own difficulty in integrating different viewpoints, or their problems in simply talking to one another. It may be possible to look at some of the family dynamics when the workers are gathered together, although this is difficult to do just before a court case. Investigating how the family pathology is repeated in the workers' interrelationships is probably better done at an earlier stage, when anxieties about what will happen in court are not predominant.

Working closely with families that have broken down means inevitably that workers become involved in the family pathology, which may impair their capacity to analyse the issues clearly for the court. Typical kinds of attitude, particularly in workers who are relatively unsophisticated about how families can create confusion in those around them, include the professional who thinks that either the family has few problems or that the parents are basically evil. Such a stark difference in views is relatively rare, but not infrequently the case with, for example, Munchausen by proxy families, where there may be a massive split between workers, reflecting the split inner world of the parent. More subtle unhelpful attitudes occur with the professional who is convinced that only his or her method of treatment can work, or who is so enmeshed with the parents that their difficulties cannot be seen clearly.

One of the main problems in this work is that it is often difficult to define clearly the nature of the work being undertaken with the family, as it involves people dealing with difficult circumstances. There are different frameworks for understanding families, and the plurality of such frameworks must be confusing for the court. Although we apply psychoanalysis in our work, we would also use whatever comes to hand with a particular family. In addition, we are usually only brought in when other kinds of treatment have already been tried and a more intensive input is required. We also usually decline to do a 'paper exercise' for courts; that is, giving an opinion on a case based soley on the documents involved, as this may be of only limited use. Seeing the family in the flesh would seem to be the best way of making a judgement about what should happen to a child; looking at the documentation comes second.

Although it is obviously good practice to attempt to examine how workers' feelings about each other may reflect family pathology, it is unfortunately often not possible to do so with outside workers in the kinds of cases treated at the Cassel. When it is possible, the treatment, though never easy, is at least relatively smooth. The more typical situation occurs as presented in the detailed case history in Chapter 5, with groups of social workers who are either basically antagonistic at heart to rehabilitation, or who cannot bear to examine in detail their own emotional reactions to very disturbed families. In the hospital, we look at staff relationships, particularly by examining the nurse–therapist relationship, the details of which are described at length in the book *The Family as In-Patient* (Kennedy et al., 1987). It is, unfortunately, too often the case that the Cassel workers feel they have to bear the brunt of the family pathology. This may include having to keep hope alive as well as facing various kinds of destructive behaviour. We have recently appointed our own social worker in an attempt to address the relationship between social services and ourselves, with some success. But there are still a number of occasions when outside workers are intractably hostile, even in the face of clear progress. Such rigid splits are obviously unhelpful, but it is unfortunately still a fact of life when working with these families.

Decision making and the treatment process itself is, then, often muddled by workers' attitudes. Making plans and having a clear focus of work is vital in this muddled and confusing field, although an obsession with planning may be merely a way of dealing with staff anxieties. Unless there has been attention to the family dynamics, a plan may be merely an invitation for detailed work to be taken apart. In view of the pressure on resources we are required more and more to justify what we are doing with a family. This usually means having to define clear goals and treatment aims. In fact, as illustrated with many cases, we do define a focus of work, which may shift as treatment proceeds, and this focus can help to define treatment goals, and so on. However, there are no guarantees in this sort of work. Our treatment programme has worked for a considerable number of families; our research has so far demonstrated our efficacy with abusing families, and we are undertaking further research into our efficacy. However, we must all be wary of being too optimistic just to deal with financial pressures and unrealistic purchasers. The judiciary can have a very important role in guiding a family towards appropriate assessment and treatment; and now have the legal backing to do so, regardless of financial anxieties put forward by local authorities. Before the landmark House of Lords judgment, judges could find ways of insisting that a family be referred to the Cassel, particularly if the Guardian ad Litem was also in favour of assessment. Local authorities are wary of taking on judges in very difficult cases, particularly when the judge takes a determined stance. However, social services departments can find ways of delaying referral, to the detriment of the family. This happened to one particular family which was denied funding for in-patient treatment, though at the court, the social services department agreed to the funding. A decision about the children's future was delayed for about a year and the social services department was censured by the experienced High Court judge, whose judgment was reported. This judgment was used as a precedent to fund families where local authorities were reluctant to do so, until the House of Lords ruling superseded it.

It is rare for us to be involved in the investigation of abuse as such, for usually the reality of the abuse has been already determined, with evidence heard in court. It has not been the aim to cover such investigations in this book, as the details are covered adequately by other writers, (see, for example, Jones, 1988). There are, however, occasions when evidence of sexual abuse only arises in the therapeutic setting, for example, in child therapy sessions. This can pose something of a dilemma, both with regard to the evidence involved and the effect that disclosures may have on treatment. Our experience is that the use of video evidence and structured interviews to elicit evidence of sexual abuse may not be adequate. Sometimes it is only within the safety of a therapeutic relationship that a child can reveal what has been going on. The necessity to take the matter further and to organize structured disclosure interviews may well interfere with the treatment process and the transference to the therapist. The treatment setting will have to be pretty firm and strong to survive such breaches of the usually protected therapeutic framework.

One of the main concerns arising in the family court is to have a clear care plan for children. When there is the prospect of rehabilitation, then this care plan will have to incorporate rehabilitation issues. For these purposes, it can be useful to divide rehabilitation into various stages, though in reality the situation with a particular family is often very complex and may not necessarily follow a neat plan, as indicated in the detailed example in Chapter 5. As illustrated in that example, once there has been an assessment recommending rehabilitation, there is then a long, slow, graded process of rehabilitation proper, with a preparatory phase usually lasting up to two months. During this time, the family prepare themselves for the reality of rehabilitation: for example, the house or flat may have to be suitably prepared, a bedroom made ready for the child, and so on. Unfortunately, there are sometimes situations when no suitable housing is available, and this may delay the rehabilitation process while the family is waiting to be rehoused. Occasionally, parents will opt out of proceeding with rehabilitation after it has been offered, once they are faced with the reality of having their child returned to them. This preparatory phase is thus a safety period, during which rehabilitation may come to an end before too much work has been undertaken. The foster placement will continue throughout this time so that, should we call a halt to treatment, the child will at least have the security of the foster home, to which they are very often significantly attached. Of course, proceeding with treatment will cause the children some confusion as well as relief, because as they begin to see more of their parents, they realize that they will have to leave their foster homes. This inevitable short-term confusion has to be weighed up against the long-term benefits of being reunited with their parents.

The first stage of rehabilitation proper, which may have to be approved by the courts, consists of a detailed plan drawn up by social services, the parent and the primary workers at the Cassel. During this stage, which usually lasts about three months, the child will gradually be introduced to the home, with brief nursed visits during the day, leading up to the first overnight un-nursed visit. By the end of this stage, the child should be on the threshold of leaving the foster home. Each part of the plan has to go well enough to proceed to the next part; sometimes the plan has to be slowed down, on the instigation of the workers or by the request of the family. Occasionally the plan has to be stopped for a while, as workers' anxiety about, for example, potential abuse, may suddenly erupt to a significant degree. It is actually rare for rehabilitation at this time to fail. Once the plan is really under way, then one has to go with it, and it usually goes well from this point on. This is not to say that there will not be crises and moments of extreme anxiety; these are inevitable. But there is usually a feeling that the treatment process can continue. There is also the fact that most of the senior staff on the Unit have seen a number of families successfully negotiate the process over the years; the staff's confidence, based on extensive experience, is an important therapeutic factor in itself. It can certainly provide a holding environment for more junior staff, particularly on the nursing side, who often have to do the face-to-face work with these difficult patients.

The second stage of rehabilitation, which also usually lasts about three months, involves the family leading up to the first full weekend at home. Soon after this, the foster placement is formally brought to an end; though, not infrequently, some informal contacts may occur, at least for a while. After the end of the foster placement, the family spend most weekends reunited in their own home.

The third stage of rehabilitation consists of a period of consolidation of the family's treatment and lasts for at least six months, and in some cases up to nine months. Before discharge, we have to be reasonably convinced that the family can survive in their own community. As discharge looms, increasing work will be undertaken to foster local networks and to prepare the family for life outside. Our experience is that it is best not to reduce the time during the week at the Cassel very much, despite the reality of discharge. We have tried such a graded end of treatment, but it is usually counterproductive. The family misses out on the vital process of ending treatment, which usually brings up important issues for them, such as fears of abandonment and feelings of vulnerability, all of which really do need to be faced rather than avoided if the rehabilitation is to succeed after discharge. However, we do encourage some extra time away from the hospital, during holiday periods, for example, as a preparation for home life, as well as some long weekends at home.

We do have follow-ups for families, depending on practicalities such as where the family live and the nature of local resources. We may also be involved with the local social services for a while, sometimes even for years, to help them think about a family following discharge. However, in general, it seems best for local resources to take on the main responsibility for the family. We are often involved when, at some point in the future, there is the wish to remove a care order, and when we may see the family to give an opinion about their readiness for this.

Although one can outline clear stages in rehabilitation, there are also situations where the early stages may be skipped over: for example, when a parent already has a child but there are significant anxieties about potential harm. Without a foster home, the initial part of rehabilitation may proceed more quickly, although there is still the need for a considerable period of consolidation. There may also be occasions when we would recommend a foster placement where none currently exists, as it may be unsafe for the child to spend unsupervised time with the parent on the weekend.

When we recommend at the initial assessment that a child be removed from the parent, we are usually required to give evidence in court to justify our decision, particularly when that decision is contested by the parent or a partner. This decision not to recommend rehabilitation is usually not an absolute recommendation, but one that proposes that the chances of success are smaller than those of failure. Generally, we look for a better than 50 per cent chance of success. However, there may be circumstances where these chances, however rough and ready our estimate of success, may be adequate as a basis for beginning rehabilitation. For example, there may not be a suitable fostering arrangement, or the foster home may have broken down and new foster parents are involved. The children may then have to be subjected to considerable disruption anyway, and so the beginning of a somewhat doubtful rehabilitation process may be justified in the face of other uncertainties. Sometimes the wishes of the children may swing the clinical judgement one way. If the children are very disturbed in their own right, a further period of uncertainty may be justified if it brings with it the possibility of a stable family arrangement.

A delicate balance may have to be drawn between giving the parents another chance and satisfying the needs of the child. A baby's needs are the most urgent, as the evidence is that adoption has a better chance of success when done at an early age. Hence, we would not want to prolong assessment with a baby involved unless we were reasonably confident of success. When the child has reached eight or nine years old, the pre-existing emotional damage may be such that there may be no significant additional harm in prolonging an assessment.

The kinds of situations which lead to our not recommending rehabilitation include: excessive violence or potential for violence, as described in the detailed clinical example in Chapter 5, when we recommended that the father was unsafe in the family; lack of willingness to engage in treatment; putting an unsatisfactory partner before the needs of the child; and a parental personality that is so emotionally damaged that any change in their parenting would simply take too long for the children's needs to be properly fulfilled. In Chapter 2, suggested detailed criteria were put forward for making judgements about the quality of parenting. The question of time needed for a parent to change is a frequent cause of concern to courts. Clinical judgements about criteria for prognosis are difficult to make; we make them on a variety of criteria as described in Chapter 2, in addition to the fact that our research findings indicate that the more able parents are to look at themselves, the more able they are to make the necessary changes. The ability of parents to accept that they have been responsible for failures within the family differs in each case. Some parents feel that admissions of failure are 'dangerous' in view of outstanding legal proceedings.

They may fear, unrealistically in fact, that such admissions would lead to our removing their children. To have a successful outcome, parents do need to acknowledge that there were problems in the family; that those problems were their fault and not the fault of some external agency; and that they needed help. Parents should not be expected to own up to everything all at once, but have to accept a level of responsibility for their actions. In order to work with parents, it is necessary to build up a relationship based on trust, with the result that it can be counterproductive to approach matters by concentrating only on certain incidents which focus on the negative aspects of parental behaviour. It is important to look for aspects of good parenting because families in these situations often feel powerless and 'put on the spot'.

When children are in the end removed from their parents, we are usually asked by the court to give an opinion about access for the parents to their children. This is often another difficult issue to deal with. One basic rule is that, in principle, there should be some kind of access, however limited, provided that this does not undermine the new placement, the long-term foster carers or adopters. In general, the local workers, who are in touch with the realities of local provisions, should be making the judgements about access. Sometimes a parent who is against adoption and seems to be uncooperative with social services, can change in their attitude once a decision is finally made by the courts. They then accept the inevitable, and it may be possible to work with them. However, it is also the case that some parents may become so embittered that they are too angry to work with professionals for the good of their children, which probably confirms the wisdom of the judgment for removal.

The question is also often asked about what further treatment should be offered to the children. There are usually short-term, medium-term and long-term treatment needs. In the short term, the children need specific help in coming to terms with the removal. We ourselves usually offer to see the children following discharge, for some brief work on their feelings about being removed from their parents. It does help the children if the parents can meet with the workers and the children, to explain that the decision was not the fault of the children, and to enable the children to feel less burdened by guilty feelings. But not all parents are able to do this difficult piece of work when they feel so bitter about the decision. Furthermore, if they were able to allow the children to go in this way, this in itself would indicate a capacity to put their children's needs to the fore, and would be more consistent with a potential for rehabilitation.

In the medium term, work will need to be undertaken to prepare the children for a long-term placement, whether fostering or adoption. Increasingly, professionals have come to realize that the more preparation, the better the chance of the adoption working. There is no ideal solution for these children, no perfect place where they will receive everything they have missed out on. There is a significant breakdown of adoption placements particularly when the adoptive parents and the children have received little preparation.

In the long term, the children may need more intensive help for long-lasting emotional and behavioural difficulties, including intensive individual psychotherapy. Unfortunately, facilities for such therapy are very variable throughout the country.

When we recommend removal of children from their parents, we are of course often subject to cross-examination in court by the parents' legal representatives. This can be a long and arduous ordeal, depending on the family's circumstances and the personalities of the presiding judge and the other lawyers. One way of attempting to nullify our clinical recommendations is to attack the Cassel treatment programme. We usually then have to explain in detail what we do. One argument frequently used against us is that the families are exposed to emotional disturbance in the hospital and that this cannot be good for them. In fact, when assessment and treatment are going satisfactorily, the children flourish in the hospital, exposed as they are to support and opportunities for stimulation. But, of course, the group of patients do have abnormal personalities. Likewise, if you are treating someone with a severe heart condition, then they may well be in a ward full of similar patients. Any drawbacks to such an environment have to be weighed against the benefits of a specialist facility.

There is the difficult issue of how much the judiciary should be aware of unconscious processes. Would such a knowledge help the decision-making process or, on the contrary, become too much of a burden? There are two main areas where such knowledge may be relevant. The first concerns the process of the hearing and the second concerns evaluation of evidence. I have never lost my sense of amazement at how decisions can be made in court, with the various sides often conferring with themselves and experts in the court corridors. What is supposed to be a rational legal procedure in fact often feels to the outsider to be totally irrational and invaded by unmodified unconscious processes. It would be preferable to meet professionals in a decent-sized room where issues can be approached in confidence and fairly rationally. The confusion in the legal process itself, with its last-minute reading of briefs and the lack of time to meet lawyers beforehand, marks the handling of these cases to the detriment of the welfare of the children.

Judges have to evaluate both evidence and character. A knowledge of psychology, whether intuitive or refined by training, must surely be relevant – particularly when they are judging the value of an expert witness. Perhaps a greater understanding of unconscious processes might be valuable to the judiciary, in order at the very least to avoid the risk that their decision making is not distorted by personal prejudices.

Despite the drawback of the court process, it is our experience that most judges are tuned into the complex issues involved in these difficult family cases. For the expert witness, it can be a useful discipline to have to give clear and precise explanations for one's opinions, with the minimum of jargon. Occasionally the duel between the expert and the various barristers can even be enjoyable. However, it is not at all certain that such remnants of the legal adversarial attitude are in the best interests of the decision-making process. Fighting in court can be a way of avoiding the complex legal and emotional issues that dealing with these difficult families entails. Improved communication between legal and mental health workers before, and during, court proceedings can only be of benefit to the children, as can increased understanding by all parties of the nature of family dynamics.

REFERENCES

Balint, M. (1968) *The Basic Fault*. London, Tavistock.

Bentovim, A. (1992) *Trauma Organized Systems, Physical and Sexual Abuse in Families*. London, Karnac Books.

Bentovim, A., Elton A., Hildebrand, J. et al. (1988) *Child Sexual Abuse within the Family: Assessment and Treatment*. London, Butterworth and Co.

Bion, W. (1959) 'Attacks on linking', *International Journal of Psychoanalysis* 40: 308–15.

Coombe, P. (1995) 'The in-patient treatment of a mother and child at the Cassel Hospital: a case of Munchausen's syndrome by proxy', *British Journal of Psychotherapy*, 12: 195–207.

Derrida, J. (1967) 'Freud and the scene of writing', in *Writing and Difference*, trans. A. Bass. London, Routledge, 1978.

Fonagy, P., Steele, H., Kennedy, R. et al. (1996) 'The relation of attachment status, psychiatric classification, and response to psychotherapy'. *J. Consult. Clin. Psychol.* 64: (1).

Freud, S. (1896) 'The aetiology of hysteria', in J. Strachey, ed., *The Standard Edition of the Complete Psychological Works of Sigmund Freud*, 24 vols. London, Hogarth, 1953–73, vol. 3, pp. 188–221.

Freud, S. (1900) 'The Interpretation of Dreams', *S.E.* 4 and 5.

Freud, S. (1901) 'The Psychopathology of Everyday Life', *S.E.* 6.

Freud, S. (1911) 'Formulations on the two principles of mental functioning', *S.E.* 12, pp. 215–26.

Freud, S. (1913) 'An evidential dream', *S.E.* 12, pp. 268–74.

Freud, S. (1930) 'Civilization and its Discontents', *S.E.* 21, pp. 57–145.

Freud, S. (1939) 'Moses and Monotheism', *S.E.* 23, pp. 2–137.

Freud, S. (1985) The complete letters of Sigmund Freud to Wilhelm Fliess, trans J. Masson, Cambridge, Mass. and London, Harvard University Press.

Fromm, E. (1974) *The Anatomy of Human Destructiveness*. London, Jonathan Cape.

Goldwyn, R. and Main, M. (1997) *Adult Attachment Scoring: A Classification System for Assessing Attachment Organization through Discourse.* Cambridge, Cambridge University Press.

Healy, K. and Kennedy, R. (1993) 'Which families benefit from in-patient psychotherapeutic work at the Cassel Hospital?' *British Journal of Psychotherapy* 9 (4): 394–404.

Healy, K., Kennedy, R. and Sinclair, J. (1991) 'Child physical abuse observed: comparison of child-abusing families and non-abusing families in an in-patient psychotherapy setting', *British Journal of Psychiatry* 158: 234–7.

James, O. (1984) 'The role of the nurse/therapist relationship in the therapeutic community', in R. Kennedy, A. Heyman and L. Tischler, eds, *The Family as In-Patient.* London, Free Association Books, 1987.

Jones, D. (1988) *Interviewing the Sexually Abused Child.* London, Gaskell.

Kennedy, R., Heyman, A. and Tischler, L. (1987) *The Family as In-Patient.* London, Free Association Books.

King, M. and Trowell, J. (1992) *Children's Welfare and the Law.* London, Sage.

Klein, M. (1957) *Envy and Gratitude.* London, Tavistock.

Lacan, J. (1966) *Ecrits.* Paris, Editions du Seuil.

Laplanche, J. (1987) *New Foundations for Psychoanalysis,* trans. D. Macey. Oxford, Blackwell, 1989.

Lynch, M. and Roberts, J. (1982) *Consequences of Child Abuse.* London, Academic Press.

Main, T. (1957) 'The Ailment', in J. Johns, ed., *The Ailment and other Psychoanalytic Essays.* London, Free Association Books, 1989.

Martin, H. (1980) 'Psychodynamic factors in child abuse', in C. Kempe and R. Helfer, eds, *The Battered Child.* Chicago: Chicago University Press.

Rosenfeld, H. (1987) *Impasse and Interpretation.* London, Tavistock.

Stern, D. (1985) *The Interpersonal World of the Child.* New York, Basic Books.

Trowell, J. (1986) 'Physical abuse of children: some considerations seen from the dynamic perspective', *Psychoanalytic Psychotherapy,* 2: 63–73.

Welldon, E. (1988) *Mother, Madonna, Whore.* London, Free Association Books.

Wilson, A. (1987) 'An outline of family work at the Cassel Hospital', in R. Kennedy, A. Heyman and L. Tischler, eds, *The Family as In-Patient.* London, Free Association Books.

Winnicott, D. (1963) *The Maturational Processes and the Facilitating Environment.* London, Hogarth Press.

Winnicott, D. (1969) 'The use of an object', in *Playing and Reality*. London, Tavistock, 1971.
Winnicott, D. (1974) 'Fear of Breakdown', *International Review of Psycho-Analysis*. 1: 103–7.

Index